HEALING POWER

HEALING POWER
Living Traditions, Global Interactions

Cunera Buijs & Wouter Welling (eds)

Published by Sidestone Press, Leiden
www.sidestone.com

Coordinator: Fanny Wonu Veys
Lay-out & cover design: Sidestone Press
Photograph cover: *Yo me lo llevo viento malo* (I ward off
the evil wind) by Santiago Rodríguez Olazábal, Cuba, 1998.
Collection NMVW no. AM-669-2 (1 t/m 3).
Chapter photographs: Mike Brink

ISBN 978-90-8890-918-4 (softcover)
ISBN 978-90-8890-919-1 (hardcover)
ISBN 978-90-8890-920-7 (PDF e-book)

Contents

7　　**List of figures**

17　　**Introduction**
Cunera Buijs and Wouter Welling

29　　**1 Invisible forces and spirits**
Cunera Buijs and Wouter Welling

32　　Getting a second pair of eyes: the precarious balance of healing and killing in Cameroon
Peter Geschiere

38　　Intimate relations between hunters and spirits in northwest Greenland
Terto Ngiviu

42　　Winti healing and the Surinamese community in the Netherlands
Marian Markelo

48　　Magical Consciousness and Healing Spirits
Susan Greenwood

57　　**2 Healing stories and images**
Cunera Buijs and Wouter Welling

60　　A Dutch way to witchcraft: the 'Wolderse Heks' from Waalre
Coby Rijkers

65　　Visions at work: when an untold story becomes a ghost
Barbara Helen Miller and Sigvald Persen

71　　Drawings in Balinese Healing and Magic
David J. Stuart-Fox

80　　Enchanted world: invisible forces and spirits
Daan van Kampenhout

87   **3 Museum magic**
             Cunera Buijs and Wouter Welling

91   Powerful things, transformations of museum objects, cases from
             the Arctic
                 Cunera Buijs

99   Roots and the art of healing
                 Anatoly Donkan and Ulrike Bohnet

104   *Kabra* healing: ancestors and colonial memory in the Netherlands
                 Markus Balkenhol

109   Shamanism in transition: ritual masks among the Piaroa
                 Claudia Augustat

117   **4 Balance and harmony**
             Cunera Buijs and Wouter Welling

120   *Aakujk'äjt-Jotkujk'äjtën:* balance and harmony in *Ayuuk* culture
                 Juan Carlos Reyes Gómez

127   Mentawai shamans in Indonesia: restoring threatened harmony
                 Reimar Schefold

133   Life Itself is a Polyrhythm – On Healing
                 Maria van Daalen

143   **5 Global interactions**
             Cunera Buijs and Wouter Welling

146   Transforming traditions: ayahuasca in the Netherlands and Peru
                 Sebastiaan van 't Holt

153   Healing music: psychedelic trance and the search for balance
                 Iris Hesse

161   Art and the Otherworld: visualizing the invisible
                 Wouter Welling

169   **About the authors**

List of figures

Figure 1 Portrait of a Mossi ritual specialist in Faka, near Kaya. The leather headband with kauri shells is a sign of consecration and dignity; he is wearing power objects. Photo: Dr. J.T. Broekhuijse, 1974. NMVW no. TM-20010354.

Figure 2 *Erzuli Dantor* by E. Lindor, Haïti, end 20th century. Papier-mâché, 60 x 22 x 15 cm. NMVW no. AM-670-3. Photo: Ferry Herrebrugh.

Figure 3 Left, the shaman Qingailisaq wearing his spirit-inspired parka. The photograph (left) is reproduced by courtesy of the Mystic Seaport Museum, Mystic CT, USA. The media photograph (right) shows the KTZ design modelled on the fashion runway during the KTZ show at the London Collections: Men AW15 at The Old Sorting Office on 11 January 2015. Photo: Tristan Fewings/Getty Images.

Figure 4 *The Apparition of the Blue and Red Deer.* Visions of Huichol mythology can be inspired by the use of hallucinogenic peyote (híkuri). After José Benitez Sanchez, Mexico, before 1988. Wool in beeswax on plywood, 60 x 60 cm. NMVW no. TM-5212-2. Photo: Irene de Groot.

Figure 5 *Bakru* by Remy Jungerman, Netherlands, 2012. Wood, textile, paper, plastic, plant material, 220 x 300 x 38 cm. NMVW no. AM-701-2a. Photo: Irene de Groot.

Figure 6 *Cascade and Hummingbirds – After Martin Johnson Heade* by Edouard Duval-Carrié, USA, 2013. Glitterglue on aluminium, 243,8 × 365,8 cm. NMVW no. AM-708-2.

Figure 7 *Ngoun le Sorcier. Chaque nuit il tue les enfants qui ont un avenir meilleur* by Art Prince, Cameroon, 1996. Paint on plywood, 40 x 69,5 cm. NMVW no. TM-5723-11. Photo: Irene de Groot.

Figure 8 *Arrestation du sorcier* by Bollo (Saturnin Wamba Djoumessi), 1990-1991. The painting shows a scene where the police uses a woman as bait to capture a man who abused his magical powers to rape and murder women in Yaoundé (Cameroon). Paint on plywood, 97 x 112 cm. NMVW no. AM-664-1. Photo: Irene de Groot.

Figure 9 Bilongo medicine bag of a traditional healer. Diola, Senegal. This bag –
probably an old army bag – contains mostly animal parts. It was collected
by father H.Govers, from the Congregation of the Holy Spirit (the Spiritines,
founders of the Afrika Museum in Berg en Dal) during his work in Senegal.
It belonged to an important ritual specialist, a blacksmith and lepra doctor
who was baptized. After his death in 1965 Father Govers was able to buy the
bag from the family. Normally it would have been burned or buried with the
deceased, but since he was baptized, a bag with rubbish was placed in the grave
instead. NMVW no. AM-63-38 (1 t/m 29). Photo: Ferry Herrebrugh.

Figure 10 *Inuk woman with a polar bear* by Buuti Petersen, West Greenland, 2011.
Acrylic on leather, 60 x 60 cm. NMVW no. RV-6146-5. Photo: Ben Grishaver.

Figure 11 *Qadruhuaq, the mysterious helper* by Simon Tookoome, Qamani'tuaq
(Baker Lake), 1972. A hunter is assisted by a mysterious creature, half fish, half
caribou. Print, 69 × 102 cm. NMVW no. RV-6094-185. Photo: Ben Grishaver.

Figure 12 Marian Markelo, winti-healer, as seen in the film interview in the exhibition *Healing Power*, 2019, Leiden. Photo: Ben Bekooy.

Figure 13 Prapi. A ceramic bowl, decorated with the snake (papa) fodu, a winti
spirit, and especially used for a herbal bath for protection or healing, Surinam,
2008. 34 x 50 x 50 cm. NMVW no. TM-6395-18.

Figure 14 A sick Maron woman seeks healing at an obiaman, who has put herbs
in a wooden dish between them. Photographer unknown, Surinam, period
1900-1930. NMVW no. TM-60005976.

Figure 15 Red menstrual drum that is ridden like a horse to guide shamanic
journeys, red, white and black spider rattle for creating connections in magical
consciousness, and black ancestor rattle to connect with deep spirit wisdom.
Photo: Susan Greenwood.

Figure 16 Part of horse rattle – my spirit guide that takes me into the realm of the
dead – used in healing sessions. The shell indicates the circular notion of interconnectedness of all life and death in the right-brain hemisphere's orientation. Photo: Susan Greenwood.

Figure 17 One of my sacred ancestors who dwells deep in the spirit Otherworld
(made by and gifted to me by shaman Gordon 'the toad' MacLellan). Photo:
Susan Greenwood.

Figure 18 Deeper into the healing issue through many levels of right-brain orientation consciousness where indications of what the problem might be lie. Insights
in this realm are arrived at through intuition rather than analysis, which comes
later when I return to everyday reality. Photo: Susan Greenwood.

Figure 19 *Yo me lo llevo viento malo* (*I ward off the evil wind*) by Santiago Rodríguez
Olazábal, Cuba, 1998. This installation by the Cuban regla de ifá babalawo
(priest) and artist Olazábal shows a healing ritual. The babalawo (right)
cleanses his patient (left) with a substance that is charged with power by the

ritual objects on the beam. Among these objects is a broom that refers to Congo roots; there it is a *mpiya*, which is used by the *nganga* (the ritual specialist) to treat someone sick by warding off evil influences. The crossroads in front is a meeting point between this and the other world. Various materials, wood, textile, plastic, earth, candles and drawings in paper. 225 × 395 × 180cm. NMVW no. AM-669-2 (1 t/m 3). Photo: Mike Bink.

Figure 20 Coby Rijkers at her home, holding one of her owls. Taken from the film interview in the exhibition *Healing Power*, Leiden 2019. Photo: Ben Bekooy.

Figure 21 Mandrake. Photo: Ben Bekooy.

Figure 22 Overview of the showcase of Coby Rijkers in the Healing Power exhibition. Photo: Ben Bekooy.

Figure 23 Sámi drum by A. Sunna, Tärnaby, Sweden, 1976. Animal skin, wood, reindeer antler. NMVW no. RV-6072-20. Photo: Irene de Groot.

Figure 24 Sámi *noaidi* with his drum and subsequently in trance, as illustrated in Johannes Schefferus's Lapponia, 1673, Frankfurt, Christian Wolff, page 139. Courtesy University Library Leiden.

Figure 25 Cupping by Sigvald Persen.

Figure 26 The upper drawing of the upside-down demon Sungsang Kala is an amulet to protect a house (*tumbal umah*); it must be hung up above the doorway. The bottom-left drawing called Essence (Sari) of Mpu Bhawula, is 'protector of the soul' (*pangraksa jiwa*), thus of life itself. Very superior since it is the gift of the deity Sanghyang Mrajapati, anyone using this formula/drawing (*aji*) will not be punished or defeated by a 'person of power' (*manusa sakti*), suggesting that the drawing may be used as protection against sorcery. The drawing can be placed in a sash or carried (as an amulet). The third nameless drawing is likewise a 'protector of the soul' (it is a common purpose) and 'remover of the efficacy of an object of sorcery' (*pamunah papasangan*); the mantra calls on the deity 'Reverser of Desti', *desti* being a form of sorcery. Bali, probably 1935-1945, ink on paper, 34 x 21,5 cm. NMVW no. RV-4844-16; Hooykaas 1980a illustration no. 53, 196-197. Photo: Irene de Groot.

Figure 27 This highly complex drawing is called Sanghyang Candi Kusumaraja, a wrathful form (*pamurtian*) of Sanghyang Andhrawang. In Balinese iconography the wrathful form is indicated by multiple bodies, here three diminishing in size one above the other, and by multiple heads. The drawing is said to be very powerful. The purpose of the drawing and its method of use is not indicated; the practitioner would decide for himself. Bali, probably 1935-1945, ink on paper, 34 x 21,5 cm. NMVW no. RV-4844-48; Hooykaas 1980a illustration no. 227. Photo: Irene de Groot.

Figure 28 This superb drawing Geni Salambang portrays an immense coiling *naga* serpent whose head is in the form of a three-headed demonic figure, as if the serpent tale emerges from its midriff. Fire issues from all over body and tail, hence its name meaning perhaps something like 'Fire portrayed'. It is said to be a 'cover of the world' (*panangkeb jagat*), suggesting protection; but also a *pangrong*, in the translation of Christiaan Hooykaas (1980b, 207) a way 'to rob (an enemy of invulnerability)', 'to avert (bullets)', or 'a means to acquire control (of another's body)'; or 'a means to capture something or someone' (*pangjukan*). Its potential for either sorcery or its eradication is indicated by the accompanying mantra: "ONG, ... your legs are unable to walk, your hands are unable to hold, for I am Fire Portrayed, Fire of the World. Your ears are unable to hear, your mouth is unable to talk, your nose is unable to smell." It is to be used in a sash, as 'protector of life', drawn on yellow silk. Bali, probably 1935-1945, ink on paper, 34 x 21,5 cm. NMVW no. RV-4844-113; Hooykaas 1980a illustration no. 315. Photo: Irene de Groot.

Figure 29 This fine drawing of two intertwined *naga* serpents is called Kaputusan Sanghyang Mretyujana, the 'Perfection of the deity Man of Death'(?). The mantra reads: "ONG Sanghyang Mretyujana blazes out from the fontanel, for I carry off the souls of many 'witches' (*leyak*), not seen by [?]... all are burned up, ya devoured by Sanghyang Mretyujana, ya all bend their knees in defeat, come be silent (*mona*) x3, come let it be so (*poma*) x3." (A *leyak* is believed to be a spirit being created through sorcery or a transformation of the sorcerer). It is to be used in a sash (or amulet); if it is not for siblings, grandchildren or parents (in other words, close family), it should not be given (used), otherwise you would be cursed by it. Bali, probably 1935-1945, ink on paper, 34 x 21,5 cm. NMVW no. RV-4844-116; Hooykaas 1980a illustration no. 301. Photo: Irene de Groot.

Figure 30 Shaman's coat, Yakut, Siberia, 1800-1830. Leather, iron, sinew, 134 x 150 cm. NMVW no. RV-1-1582. Photo: Ben Grishaver.

Figure 31 Belt by Daan van Kampenhout. Photo: Daan van Kampenhout.

Figure 32 Bird costume by Daan van Kampenhout. Photo: Daan van Kampenhout.

Figure 33 Bilongo, power object. Container of a strong spiritual force that can be used as protection against diseases or to ward off evil influences. The mirror functions as a window through which the spirit can look outside or the nganga (ritual specialist) can find the cause of the disease. It usually contains natural materials such as white and red earth, bones, resin, seeds. Congo, end 19th century, 10 x 21 x 71 cm. NMVW no. WM-3018. Photo: Irene de Groot.

Figure 34a Shaman's drum, Nivkh, Southeast Siberia, 1850-1898. Animal skin, wood, 74 x 63 cm. NMVW no. RV-1202-239. Photo: Irene de Groot.

Figure 34b A shaman is treating a sick woman sitting on the sleeping platform. From: Leopold von Schrenck: Reisen und Forschungen im Amur-Lande in den Jahren 1854-1856. Band III. Pl-LXI no. 4. St.Petersburg, K.Akademie der Wissenschaften. 1881. Courtesy Royal Library, The Hague, Netherlands.

Figure 35 Grass doll used to take away sickness, Oroch, Southeast Siberia,1875-1898. 6,3 x 15 x 34 cm. RV-1202-96. Photo: Ben Grishaver.

Figure 36 Anatol Donkan wearing the shaman's coat he made. The costume is now in the collection of the National Museum of World Cultures, Leiden, 2017. Salmon and catfish leather, iron and copper, ink, 148 x 158 cm. NMVW no. 7143-1 t/m 4. Photo: Christine Fottner.

Figure 37 Shaman's coat by Anatol Donkan, 2017, on display in the healing exhibition in 2019, Leiden. Salmon and catfish leather, iron and copper, ink, 148 x 158 cm. NMVW no. 7143-1 t/m 4. Photo: Ben Bekooy.

Figure 38 Portrait of Anatoly Donkan. Photo: Christine Fottner.

Figure 39 House-spirit 'grandmother' by Anatoly Donkan, , Germany, 2018. Wood, glass, textile, 44 × 28 × 28 cm. NMVW no. 7143-6. Photo: Irene de Groot.

Figure 40 Anatoly Donkan is drawing mythical designs on the shaman's coat which he made for the National Museum of World Cultures in Leiden, Netherlands. Photo: Christine Fottner.

Figure 41 Shaman's belt, Oroch, Southeast Siberia, from the Adolph Dattan collection of the National Museum of World Cultures, Leiden. 1850-1898. Leather, iron, 28,8 x 98,5 cm. NMVW no. RV-1202-235. Photo: Irene de Groot.

Figure 42 Yoruba Egungun mask representing an ancestor. West-Africa, date unknown. Wood, iron, 9 cm x 17,5 cm x diam. 20,5 cm. NMVW no. AM-481-5. Photo: Ferry Herrebrugh.

Figure 43 Kabra ancestor mask by Boris van Berkum, 2013. Lacquered polyurethane, batik textile, wood, 66 x 40 x 40 cm. Amsterdam Museum Collection. Amsterdam. Photo: Erik Hesmerg.

Figure 44 Kabra ancestor dance mask performs during the libation by Marian Markelo in the Oosterpark in Amsterdam, 2013, at the National Commemoration of the 150th anniversary of the abolition of slavery. Photo: James van den Ende.

Figure 45 Mama Aisa by Boris van Berkum, 2020. Marian Markelo posed for this sculpture. Polyesther with goldleaf 150 x 100 x 125 cm. Computer render.

Figure 46 Headdress. Piaroa, Venezuela, South-America. Before 1968, feathers, plant materials, 70 × 25 × 29cm. NMVW no. TM-3764-6. Photo: Irene de Groot.

Figure 47 Model of a mask dancer. Piaroa, Venezuela, South-America. Made before 1999. Photo: Claudia Augustat.

Figure 48 Atelier of artist Alfonso Peres in Paria Grande, Venezuela. 1999. Photo: Claudia Augustat.

Figure 49 Set for snuffing *yopo*. Collection Augustat, Piaroa, Venezuela, South-America, 2000. Photo: Claudia Augustat.

Figure 50 The ghost of the peccari and the monkey are part of the original masks created by Wahari. Mask of the monkey spirit. Piaroa, Venezuela, South-America. Before 1968, plant materials, 80 × 30 × 20cm. NMVW no. TM-3764-18. Photo: Irene de Groot.

Figure 51 Young Mentawaian shaman with ornaments, Indonesia, 1895 Photo: C.B. Nieuwenhuis, 1895. NMVW no. TM-10005477.

Figure 52 Skirt of a shaman, Sakudei, Indonesia, ca. 1950. Cotton, mother-of-pearl, rotan, feathers, 58 × 58cm, NMVW no. 7086-128. Photo: Irene de Groot.

Figure 53 Depositing offerings to the Ayuuk gods before an altar, at the priest's house, asking for care and protection. Photo: Juan Carlos Reyes Gómez.

Figure 54 Blouse, made by the Kojpëtë, a weaving and dyeing school in the Mixe (Ayuuk) town of Tlahuitoltepec Oaxaca Mexico. Cotton, machine embroidered. 2016, 70 × 148cm. NMVW no. 7098-1. Photo: Irene de Groot.

Figure 55 Blouse designed by Isabel Marant, based on the original Mixe blouse. Spring/summer collection 2015. The designer was accused of cultural appropriation. Cotton, wool, machine embroidered. 2015. 97 × 155cm. NMVW no. 7043-1. Photo: Irene de Groot.

Figure 56 Family giving an offering to the Ayuuk gods, on top of I'px Yuukm, to thank that the year he served the community, as an authority, there were no problems. Photo: Juan Carlos Reyes Gómez.

Figure 57 Shaman's headband (sorot or luat). A broad strip of split rattan is wrapped in fabric and decorated in a patterned arrangement with strings of glass beads. Added to the headband are decorated little rods that are placed behind the ears. Glass beads, bebeget rattan, cotton fabric, chicken feathers, vegetative material, mother-of pearl. Siberut, Mentawai, Indonesia, 1950. 20 × 19 × 30 cm. NMVW no. 7086-13. Photo: Irene de Groot.

Figure 58 A 'seeing' shaman expels harmful forces from the communal house during a nocturnal ritual in the Sakuddei uma. 1967. Photo Reimar Schefold.

Figure 59 Adorned shaman dancing with *abak ngalou* pendant, *toggoro* loincloth and *sabo* dancing apron. 1978. Photo Reimar Schefold.

Figure 60 Shaman's chest. Mentawai, Indonesia, ca. 1950. Wood, rotan. 17 × 65 × 16 cm. NMVW TM-5769-1. Photo: Irene de Groot.

Figure 61 Shaman's wife, with festive *teteku* ornament. Mentawai, Indonesia, 1978. Photo Reimar Schefold.

Figure 62 In my *badji* or altar-room are altars for several groups of *Lwa-yo* ('angels' or 'mysteries' in Haitian Vodou): white for Rada, red for Petro, golden for Papa Loko and Legba (corner), purple for Ghede (floor). I serve the *Lwa* with drinks, food, lighted candles, flowers, songs, etc. On the floor a special *sevis* (service) for Papa Ogou, with two machetes.
Interesting, in this photo also a service for a *keris pusaka* (floor). This is not Haitian Vodou but part of the Indonesian tradition. The Dutch-Indonesian connection has its roots in colonial times. 2020. Photo: Maria van Daalen.

Figure 63 An oil lamp is made for a certain *Lwa*. This *lamp* is for Manbo Erzulie Freda, to help a client in a love situation. Ingredients can be olive oil, pink rose petals, perfume, certain herbs (in the oil), and of course a wick. Once the *lamp* is lighted, it has to burn continuously for a certain amount of days. 2020. Photo: Maria van Daalen.

Figure 64 This *vévé* is made by Maria van Daalen. A *vévé* is traced in cornflour and is a portal for a certain *Lwa* ('angel' or 'mystery' in Haitian Vodou). There are many different *vévé*'s. This one is for Legba who 'opens the door'. Added to it are three stars, a design with two crossed v's, and the candle and mug (in cornflour). All designs are traditional. The *vévé* is activated with a lighted candle, with food (sugarcane e.o.), with drinks, and with certain songs. The eight shawls or *mouswa* in seven colors plus white, symbolize all the *Lwa*. 2020. Photo: Maria van Daalen.

Figure: 65 *Agwe* by Pierrot Barra (1942-1999). Agwe is a *Lwa* (spirit) from the sea, depicted as an admiral or captain of the ship Imamou which is taking the dead to their ancestral homes. Haïti. Plastic dolls, fabrics, various materials, 63,5 x 110 x 117 cm. NMVW no. AM-681-14. Photo: Ferry Herrebrugh.

Figure: 66 *Agwe* (part of the installation *Le Monde des Ambaglos – The World of the Underwater Beings* which consists of three *Lwa* in three boats: Mambo Inan, Agwe and Erzulie) by Edouard Duval-Carrié, Haïti, 2007-08. Polyester, various materials, 255 x 95 x 300 cm (boat; incl. the long arms of Agwe 500 cm). NMVW no. AM-681-2a.

Figure 67 *L' anniversaire de Damballah* (*Damballah's Birthday*) by Préfète Duffaut, 2007, Haïti. Painting on canvas, 103 x 103 cm. NMVW no. AM-681-8. Photo: Irene de Groot.

Figure 68 *The Last Supper* by Frantz Augustin Zéphirin. The twelve apostles surrounded by *Lwa* (spirits) from the vodou pantheon. Haïti, 2001. Acrylic on canvas, 76 x 101 cm. NMVW no. AM-670-2. Photo: Ferry Herrebrugh.

Figure 69 *Cosas del espiritu 2* by Santiago Rodríguez Olazábal, 1998. In an early age the artist was initiated in the Oshún cult; he is a Santería/Regla de Ifa priest. His work is strongly related to this African diaspora religion. Cuba. Mixed techniques on paper, 88 x 67 cm. NMVW no. AM-606-18. Photo: Ferry Herrebrugh.

Figure 70 Diogenes Garcia amidst the chacruna plant. On his shirt is the image of the plant's leaf, together with the head of a serpent and a cross-section of the ayahuasca vine. Above that is a rectangle of patterns, as they are observed in ayahuasca visions. His corona (hat) is now part of the museum's collection. Peru, 2018. Photo: Sebastiaan van 't Holt.

Figure 71 Every morning Mama Rosa prepares different mixtures of plants. I asked a collaborator of the ayahuasca centre if he drinks it. He answers: 'No, I enjoy my sleep more lately'. Peru, 2018. Photo: Sebastiaan van 't Holt.

Figure 72 Shaman's costume (*Kushma*). Luis Marquez wore this costume while he was leading ayahuasca ceremonies. The serpent transfers his wisdom to the ceramic bowl that will contain that knowledge for the Shipibo culture. During ayahuasca ceremonies Luis Marquez has visions. He communicates these visions with his wife. Based on his stories she has created this cotton costume in six months' time. Luis Marquez explains: "Left you can see a *tinaja*, related to the festivities of the Shipibo and purple coloured chacruna leaves that give me life. Ayahuasca enables us to maintain our culture in spite of all the problems that we as Shipibo encounter. On the right a green anaconda is depicted who provides me wisdom, also about establishing a school for the Shipibo children." Peru, Pucallpa, Shipibo, 2018. NMVW no. 7163-1. Photo: Irene de Groot.

Figure 73 Medical plant (*Llanten*) by Dimas Paredes Armas. Children's bronchitis is treated with *Llanten*. This is one of the plants the Shipibo find in their backyards or in the surrounding forests. Gouache, 32,5 x 38,5 cm. Peru, Pucallpa, Shipibo. 2011. NMVW no. 7163-6c). Photo: Irene de Groot.

Figure 74 Shaman Antonio Vasquez postures with his pipe in front of the *maloka* (ceremonial space). Peru; 2018. Photo: Miriam Moreno.

Figure 75 Psy-fi Festival in Leeuwarden, the Netherlands. Shamanic elements can be seen during the festival and the clothing of the festival goers is inspired by non-Western cultures. The participants listen and react in their own way to the DJ and the music. 2018. Photo: Iris Hesse.

Figure 76 Another way to reach a meditative state of mind is to make string-art. This image shows the result of one of the Rotoris workshops. This art decorates the psytrance festivals to enhance the experience of the visitors. 2018. Photo: Iris Hesse.

Figure 77 Psy-fi Festival in Leeuwarden, the Netherlands. The community gathers at a heavily decorated stage. Nature elements prevail; at the centre is a world tree (axis mundi), which is symbolic of nature (Mother Earth). Their outfits are loose fitting, comfortable organic clothing that allow the participants to dance freely and let themselves go. Sometimes their wardrobes are inspired by non-Western cultures. High quality speakers are proportionally and efficiently placed to disperse the rhythmic beats and hypnotizing waves over the gathered public. In a sense, these elements can create a state of trance, which can linger on and enable people to dance for hours on end. 2018. Photo: Iris Hesse.

Figure 78 The film recordings made by Iris Hesse in the exhibition Healing Power in Leiden, 2019. On the right the sculpture *Princess of Trance* by the Belgian artist Bart van Dijck.

Figure 79a *The artist is present* by Marina Abramović. Video registration of the performance in MoMA, New York, 2010. Courtesy Marina Abramović Institute.

Figure 97b *The artist is present* by Marina Abramović in the exhibition *Healing Power*, Leiden 2019. Photo: Ben Bekooy.

Figure 80a Mathilde ter Heijne lightens the candles of her work *Send it back to where it came from*, 2010. Leiden, 28 juni 2019. Photo: Wouter Welling.

Figure 80b *Send it back where it came from* by Mathilde ter Heijne, 2010. Metal, wax, 150 x 125 x 125 cm. Collection of the artist. Photo: Christine Dierenbach.

Figure 81 Exhibition room *Between worlds* in the exhibition *Healing Power*, Leiden 2019. At the left *Fin* by Johan Tahon, 2004-2014, plaster. Photo: Ben Bekooy.

Figure 82 *Imposición de manos* (*Laying on of hands*) by José Bedia, U.S.A., ca.2013. Pigment on amate paper, 121 x 242 cm.. NMVW no. AM-708-1. Photo: Irene de Groot.

Figure 83 *Incantation #6 – The Alchemy of Healing* by Renée Stout, 2015. Acrylic on canvas, glass, rhinestones. 45,7 x 180,3 x 0,3 cm. Courtesy Renée Stout & Hemphill Gallery, Washington DC. NMVW no. 7164-1a. Photo: Irene de Groot.

Introduction

Cunera Buijs and Wouter Welling

Aim of this publication

People around the world are seeking out new and alternative forms of spirituality and healing, and they do so not in isolation but in global interactions. Cultural contacts prevail, cultures intermingle, and new forms of spirituality and healing are created as part of broader processes of cultural dynamics.

In many societies around the world, including in the West, these topics are intriguing and highly relevant; they play an important role in the revival of culture and identity. In 2019, the National Museum of World Cultures in Leiden organized a thematic exhibition on spiritual healing practices globally. The exhibition 'Healing Power, Winti, Shamanism and More' opened in July 2019 and closed its doors on the 6th of January 2020. A second venue will take place at the Tropenmuseum in Amsterdam in 2021-2022. Prior to the exhibition we organized an expert meeting of ritual specialists, scientists and artists in the field of healing, shamanism, Vodou[1], Winti and witchcraft. The articles in this publication are based on the discussions held during this two-day meeting in May 2017, complemented with additional contributions.

Historically there has been extensive scientific interest in the lifestyles, knowledge, cultures, histories, worldviews and religions of indigenous peoples. Great museums and universities worldwide have built magnificent collections of indigenous art and objects related to spirituality. These collections and ritual practices related to healing are often a concern for many indigenous peoples because of the potential for transgressing the sacred and codes of secrecy. Outsiders often find it difficult to determine what should stay hidden and what is permissible for public viewing. Today indigenous peoples continue to fight for their rights, not only for their land,

Sokari Douglas Camp: part of the sculpture *Freud*
White Sacrifice, 1998, collection of the artist.

cultural heritage and language but also for their indigenous knowledge, spiritual culture and healing practices.

In the urbanized, secularized West, culture has lost contact with healing traditions and religious customs. There is a separation of nature and culture, as well as divisions between material and spiritual, or material and immaterial, that contribute to a romanticized notion of nature. At the same time, there is also a lively fascination with alternative healing practices and neo-paganism, which can provide a feeling of connectedness to nature and the spiritual world, dissolving the border between material and immaterial, or between body and mind or soul. This leads to highly sophisticated discourses, even more when Indigenous philosophies are concerned. Similarly, the poetics and translations of artists inspired by, experiencing or reflecting on spiritual healing and other spiritual worlds also generate much interest (see Clifford 2013).

But the derivation of healing practices from external cultural traditions happens not only in the West; partly because colonization robbed so many of their spiritual context, Indigenous peoples around the world have found inspiration in foreign cultural traditions as well (see Jakobsen 1999; Hutton 2001; Vitebsky 2001; Jespers 2009). And their descendants develop new ways to connect both to their ancestors and to new healing practices. In this publication we explore a small selection of the manifold healing practices found in the world and offer introductions to what they mean for individuals or communities.

This book draws together articles from ritual specialists, (indigenous) artists and scientists active in spiritual healing practices worldwide. Art and powerful objects, and their role within a museum context, are explored, and the authors reflect on the museum's collections. Their perspectives, coming from many different directions and experiences, are inspiring and innovative, and should be of interest to readers everywhere. In *Healing Power, Living Traditions, Global Interactions* several authors from the field introduce the topic of healing and spirituality, and define and compare spiritual healing, shamanism, neo-shamanism, Indigenous medicine and Western healing music. In these articles, and riddles and contrasts between Western reductionism and holistic worldviews are explored, and the authors shed light on 'spiritual healing' in relation to both individual illnesses and the collective traumas of the (colonial) past. Finally, the contributions elaborate upon cultural appropriation and the dissolution of borders, placing these in relation to the dynamic process of global interactions.

The role of ritual specialists and healers in society

Nowadays, the term 'shaman' is widely known and used to refer to a broad range of ritual specialists from around the world, from Siberia, where the term stems from, to South America, the United States and Europe. However, the denomination 'shaman', is complicated because it encompasses many different specialists, including witches, priests, magic doctors, medicine men, healers, conjurers, dream interpreters. Each culture employs specific terms to refer to these. The word 'shaman' derives from the language of the Tungus, a Siberian people; '*šaman/ša*' means 'knowing' and 'shaman' is 'someone who knows'. Related to the Sanskrit '*sramana*' and similar to the Chinese '*sha-men*', which means 'he who is in ecstasy' (see Vitebsky 2001, 6ff; Hutton 2001, 47ff; Walter and Fridmann 2004, XXI), the term has been adopted into

Figure 1 Portrait of a Mossi ritual specialist in Faka, near Kaya. The leather headband with kauri shells is a sign of consecration and dignity; he is wearing power objects.
Photo: Dr. J.T. Broekhuijse, 1974. NMVW no. TM-20010354.

many languages. The British historian Ronald Hutton, who researched British pre-Christian religions and folklore as well as neo-paganism, Wicca, witchcraft and shamanism, explains in his book on Siberian shamanism that, although the term 'shaman' stems from a Siberian language, it has evolved following Western taste and Euro-American culture. Because of this, Hutton (2001, VII) argues, the word 'shaman' as we use it today is a Western construct and simplification. We would add that the many words for shamans and ritual specialists that exist in different languages can hardly be translated into one general term, as they refer to the specific roles that ritual specialists perform in their own communities. The shaman, priest, medicine man, witch – all of them fulfil expectations of their community. What we can generalize is this: they are expected to 'know' more than the average person in the community and get this additional knowledge by mediating between realms.

Peter de Smet, who as a clinical pharmacologist conducted research in Africa, makes clear in his book *Herbs, Health, Healers* that traditional medical practices are far from understood (1999, 8). He writes:

In any place and time, conceptions of healing and diseases . . . are rooted in fundamental ideas of life itself. This means that one has to study the African view of life. . . . Everything is invested with a life force . . . all of which have their own personality and cosmic place. It is common to see an African healer talking to a tree so that he may control and use the life force within for the benefit of his patient (De Smet 1999, 12).

In many traditions where people and nature are closely connected, the experience of life and the world is holistic, meaning that there is no distinction made between spiritual and non-spiritual (physical). There is no division between the visible and non-visible; borders are blurred between death and life, as well as between human beings and animals or spirits. Ancestors, (animal) spirits and gods can inspire and inform via dreams and visions. They shed light on the causes of imbalance and illness, and advise on treatment and how to re-establish harmony.

Colonialism, Christianity and the marginalization of traditions
Though cultural exchange has long existed, through trade relations in pre-colonial times, the African diaspora religions are a result of colonization. Colonial rulers – plantation owners, missionaries – suppressed indigenous religions, customs and healing practices in the countries they occupied and the people they enslaved. Colonists characterized local religions as idolatry and superstition stemming from the devil. Since the people made slaves on the plantations in the Americas were not allowed to practise their Vodun religion, they adopted parts of Christianity and mixed these with their own practices, bringing together Christian saints and spirit beings. Catholic imagery was used as camouflage for their own spirituality (see Hübner and

Welling: 2009). An example is the iconic representation of mother and child, looking like Mary and Jesus, but actually depicting the Haitian mother-goddess Erzuli Dantor and her daughter Anaïs.

Political regimes like the atheistic communism prevailing in the former Soviet Union also had a destructive influence in some regions on spirituality and healing traditions. Shamans were accused of being *'kulaks'*, the rich and powerful in Siberian society, and were persecuted and put in prison. Shamans were known for their abilities to fly – an idea related to the 'shaman's spiritual journey' – so, Soviet officials forced them to show their skills and threw them out of helicopters. Their costumes and drums were burned, or confiscated and transferred to major anthropological museums in Russia (Hutton 2001, 25).

Prosecution and suppression of pre-Christian religions occurred also in Europe. Best known are the witch trials that reached their peak between 1560-1630, but lasted till the late eighteenth century (Hutton 1999, 379). In continental Europe, the British Isles and the North American colonies, around one hundred thousand

Figure 2 *Erzuli Dantor* by E. Lindor, Haïti, end 20th century. Papier-mâché, 60 x 22 x 15 cm. NMVW no. AM-670-3. Photo: Ferry Herrebrugh.

trials took place, of which approximately half resulted in conviction, 'leading to punishments that included not only shaming, imprisonment and banishment, but also, more often, hanging, beheading and burning' (Gaskill 2018, 97). Eighty percent of the suspects were women.

Globalization

Despite the suppression of other traditions, the West's fascination with spiritual cultures never completely disappeared. Europeans found inspiration in ancient Egypt and were also inspired by eastern cultures (Orientalism). To find traces of their own historical spiritual religions, the Icelandic sagas were rediscovered. At several moments in the history of Western societies there has been a longing for holistic experience and for a spirituality lost to time. For example, in D.H. Lawrence's novel *The Plumed Serpent* (first published in 1926) one of his protagonists sighs:

> So if I want the Mexicans to learn the name of Quetzalcoatl, it is because I want them to speak with the tongues of their own blood. I wish the Teutonic world would once more think in terms of Thor and Wotan, and the tree Iggdrasil. And I wish the Druidic world would see, honestly, that in the mistletoe is their mystery, and that they themselves are the Tuatha De Danaan, alive, submerged. (Lawrence [1926] 1950, 261)

Lawrence writes of the return to the Western spiritual sources, yet such wisdom was mostly sought elsewhere. The East was popular: upon Krishnamurti was forced the role of guru, which he refused. In the 1960s, there was a surge of interest in eastern philosophy. The Beatles went to India and visited Maharishi Mahesh Yogi, and many young Europeans found their way to Buddhism. The musical *Hair* (1969) announced the New Age with the lyrics 'This is the dawning of the Age of Aquarius'. At the turn of the twenty-first century, Westerners interested in spiritual traditions from other parts of the world looked even further: Vodou, with African roots; shamanism, in Siberian, Mongolian and North American traditions; Santo Daime and ayahuasca, with Brazilian and Peruvian origins. The roots of Western spiritual, pre-Christian traditions were rediscovered in neo-paganism, with many taking up Wicca and traditional witchcraft (see Greenwood 2000; Jespers 2009; Hutton 1999). As individual freedom is the paradigm of the twenty-first century, sometimes elements from different traditions are combined. The dogmatic and rigid interpretations by abuse-inflicted religious systems have been replaced by personal experience whether or not in a communal setting (see St John 2011).

Influence of tourism

Outside South America, the ceremonial substance ayahuasca has become known through the Santo Daime church, a religious community that organizes ceremonies all over the world, including in the Netherlands. In recent years, ayahuasca has developed such popularity that dedicated centres have mushroomed. Touristic participation in ayahuasca ceremonies has increased, especially in Peru where for centuries ayahuasca has been an important part of spiritual life. Some local shamans, *curanderos*, now work exclusively with tourists. This aggravates their own communities who often criticise them, at times understandably, as some turn the ritual into a show and are jokingly called 'Disney shamans'. In recent years, Europeans, Australians and North Americans relocate to the Amazon to do shamanic work, competing with indigenous curanderos in the process. Tourists also travel to North America, Greenland, Mongolia and Siberia in search of shamans, treatments for poorly understood illnesses or social and psychological problems, and new spiritual experiences. This outside demand influences and changes local traditions and provides new sources of income. Questions arise as to whether it is acceptable to adopt spiritual sacred traditions from other cultures, and to whom these spiritual practices belong. This brings us to the topic of cultural appropriation.

Cultural appropriation: a case in Nunavut

On November 25, 2015, Canadian Broadcasting Company (CBC) Radio reported a story entitled: 'Nunavut family outraged after fashion label copies sacred Inuit design'.[2] The 'sacred design' referred to the spiritual vision of an Inuit shaman named Qingailisaq, which was graphically portrayed on a caribou-skin parka made to provide spiritual protection to him. The shaman's descendants in Nunavut, however, discovered that a high-end clothing designer, Kokon To Zai (KTZ), in the United Kingdom, had begun marketing this sacred design in the form of a commercially produced sweater.

The shaman's coat, a subject of scholarly intrigue for many years, is considered by experts to be the 'most unique garment known to have been created in the Canadian Arctic'.[3] The design, taken by KTZ without the family's consent or permission, is an obvious copy of their ancestor's parka. Salome Awa, the great-granddaughter of Qingailisaq, angrily declared: 'This is a stolen piece. There is no way that this fashion designer could have thought of this exact duplicate by himself. I was furious. I was angry. I was upset. I was in shock, most of all'.[4]

This case clearly shows that cultural appropriation, copyright and ownership issues are at stake. While artists and fashion designers may find inspiration in non-Western cultures, others, often including people from the cultures involved, do not wish to have their cultural elements used in artistic or fashion products. Such 'borrowing' becomes even more contested when it involves sacred or spiritual cultural elements. But the borderline between inspiration and appropriation is often vague and ill-defined. Interpretations of 'inspiration' and 'appropriation' vary, and individual cases can be accepted or rejected, even within the same culture.

Figure 3 Left, the shaman Qingailisaq wearing his spirit-inspired parka. The photograph (left) is reproduced by courtesy of the Mystic Seaport Museum, Mystic CT, USA. The media photograph (right) shows the KTZ design modelled on the fashion runway during the KTZ show at the London Collections: Men AW15 at The Old Sorting Office on 11 January 2015. Photo: Tristan Fewings/Getty Images.

Cultural appropriation also plays a role in New Age healing festivals, where people borrow elements, such as drumming and music from non-Western cultures, that are then combined and reshaped into new forms of spirituality and healing.

Art, artists and healing

Works of art can be inspired by the makers' spiritual experiences. Some artists are practitioners, and their art may have a healing intention. The domains of ritual specialists and visual artists have always been connected. Spiritual ways of thinking are based on abstraction, associations and symbolism. Healing, fear, hope and spirituality are linked to inspirited materials and colours.

Artists working within specific cultural traditions express their worldview and cosmology in their art. The art of the Huichol from Mexico, for example, has been amplified by the use of hallucinogenic drugs, fasting, singing, meditation and concentration. The yarn paintings of the Huichol are made under the influence of the holy peyote, a spineless cactus. The mescaline in the plant affects human consciousness, allowing users to see abstract patterns and intense colours in the yarn paintings.

Figure 4 *The Apparition of the Blue and Red Deer*. Visions of Huichol mythology can be inspired by the use of hallucinogenic peyote (híkuri). After José Benitez Sanchez, Mexico, before 1988. Wool in beeswax on plywood, 60 x 60 cm. NMVW no. TM-5212-2. Photo: Irene de Groot.

There are also artists who draw inspiration from their cultural background, while simultaneously positioning themselves within the international art world. For example, the Dutch-Surinamese visual artist Remy Jungerman has developed a visual language in which he links Surinamese Winti rituals and Maroon symbolism to Piet Mondrian's European modernism. Santiago Rodríguez Olazábal from Cuba is both a visual artist and a priest of Regla de Ifá, a religion of African origin practised in Cuba. In the installation presented in figure 19, one of the symbols, the cross, is a Congolese cosmogramme representing the stages of life. Many artists are familiar with this type of imagery. Many relate their art to other worlds and explore the space between the visible and the invisible.

Figure 5 *Bakru* by Remy Jungerman, Netherlands, 2012. Wood, textile, paper, plastic, plant material, 220 x 300 x 38 cm. NMVW no. AM-701-2a. Photo: Irene de Groot.

More than any other form of art, performance art connects to shamanic traditions. Performance art has a strong ritual character. For example, Joseph Beuys used materials based on their immaterial, spiritual essence, and Marina Abramović's performances have a magical, mesmerizing (healing, exorcistic, cleansing) quality. Beuys and Abramović both show in their work the shamanic experience and focus on a form of healing. In a sense, during their performances these artists themselves become shamans.

Concluding remarks

The scope of spirituality and healing is immense. Countless publications precede this one, which is only a limited contribution to the highly sophisticated discourse on the topic.

While organizing the Healing Power exhibition in the National Museum of World Cultures, we were criticized by the Dutch Vereniging tegen Kwakzalverij (Association against Quackery). This organization protests against alternative healing practices that are not scientifically approved. In their view, the exhibition, which dealt with Winti, Vodou, shamanism, witchcraft and other marginalized healing traditions, promoted quackery. Obviously, Western-biased misinterpretations, dominance and control still play a central role and leave little room for indigenous knowledge and philosophy. We hope to demonstrate how healers and ritual specialists, just as artists, have a role to play for the benefit of their societies. As Abramović writes in her biography *Walk through Walls*:

It's about humanity, humbleness, and collectively. It is very simple. Maybe together we can change consciousness and transform the world. And we can start doing this anywhere. (Abramović 2017, 361).

References

Abramović, Marina. 2017. *Walk Through Walls*. London: Penguin Random House UK.

Clifford, J. 2013. *Returns. Becoming Indigenous in the Twenty-First Century*. Cambridge, Massachusetts / London: Harvard University Press.

De Smet, Peter. 1999. *Herbs, Health, Healers: Africa as ethno-pharmacological treasury*. Berg en Dal: Afrika Museum.

Gaskill, Malcolm. 2018. "The Fear and Loathing of Witches." In *Spellbound: Magic, Ritual & Witchcraft*, edited by Sophie Page, Marina Wallace. Oxford: Ashmolean.

Greenwood, Susan. 2000. *Magic, Witchcraft and the Otherworld: An Anthropology*. London: Bloomsbury.

Hübner, I. and W. Welling. 2009. *Roots & more – the journey of the spirits*. Berg en Dal: Afrika Museum.

Hutton, Ronald. 1999. *The Triumph of the Moon: A History of Modern Pagan Witchcraft*. Oxford and New York: Oxford University Press.

Hutton, Ronald. 2007. *Shamans. Siberian Spirituality and the Western Imagination*. London: Hambledon Continuum.

Jakobsen, Merete Demant. 1999. *Shamanism. Traditional and Contemporary Approaches to the Mastery of Spirits and Healing*. New York / Oxford: Berghahn Books.

Jespers, Frans (ed.). 2009. *Nieuwe religiositeit in Nederland. Gevalstudies en beschouwingen over alternatieve religieuze activiteiten*. Budel: Uitgeverij DAMON.

Lawrence, D.H. 1950. *The Plumed Serpent*. Harmondsworth: Penguin Books.

Oosten, Jarich. 1997. "Amulets, shamanic clothes and paraphernalia in Inuit culture." In *Braving the cold, Continuity and change in Arctic clothing*, edited by Cunera Buijs and Jarich Oosten. Leiden: Research School CNWS, 105-131.

St John, G. 2011. "Spiritual technologies and altering consciousness in contemporary counterculture." *Altering consciousness: Multidisciplinary perspectives* 1: 203-225.

Vitebsky, Piers. 2001. *Shamanism*. Norman: University of Oklahoma Press.

Walter, M.N. and E.J. Neumann Fridmann (eds). 2004. "Introduction." In *Shamanism, An Encyclopedia of World Beliefs, Practices and Culture*. Santa Barbara: ABC-CLIO.

Notes

1   We use Vodun for the West African religion and Vodou for the Haitian religion.
2   https://www.cbc.ca/radio/asithappens/as-it-happens-wednesday-edition-1.3336554/
     nunavut-family-outraged-after-fashion-label-copies-sacred-inuit-design-1.3336560
3   https://www.cbc.ca/news/canada/north/inuit-shaman-parka-design-history-1.3345968. See also
     Oosten (1997, 120ff).
4   CBS Radio, 25 November 2015.

1 Invisible forces and spirits

Cunera Buijs and Wouter Welling

Worldwide there are spiritual traditions with ancient roots that have become interpreted and mixed in new ways in contemporary societies. One enduring notion is that there are certain places where spiritual beings or energies are manifest.

Ritual specialists mediate between the earthly realm and the spirit world. However, in a holistic worldview, the distinction between the natural and supernatural, between human beings and spirits, is non-existent. Instead, there is a complex reality in which everything is connected, and everything should be in balance. Explanations for imbalance vary, though they are often related to relationships with the ancestors and the surrounding community (see Anderson 2011, 2ff.; De Smet 1999; Vitebsky 2001).

Imbalance can only be cured with the aid of ritual specialists. With their expertise and experience, they can create a connection with the invisible world in order to restore balance. This is an act of healing, which takes place through the interaction of the healer and invisible forces.

Ideas about this invisible world are deeply rooted in closely guarded local traditions and knowledge that often relates to the surrounding landscape. In South America, for example, certain places in the landscape, such as cascades, are sacred and inhabited by spiritual beings (Miller 2015, x; Pešoutov 2019; Vitebsky 2001, 154-58).

Surinamese Winti (spirits) manifest themselves in diverse habitats like rivers, lakes, forests, earth and sky. All have their own characters and features. Though invisible, Winti influence people's lives and can affect their well-being and harmony, explains *obiman* (Winti priestess) Marian Markelo in her contribution to this chapter, which is based on her personal experience.

Figure 6 *Cascade and Hummingbirds – After Martin Johnson Heade* by Edouard Duval-Carrié, USA, 2013. Glitterglue on aluminium, 243,8 × 365,8 cm. NMVW no. AM-708-2.

Terto Ngiviu, a social scientist from Greenland, explains in her contribution the relationships between hunters and spirits there. For Inugguit hunters in Greenland today, spirits can be benevolent or frightening. They may improve the outcome of the hunt, and even be a hunter's friend, as was the case in ancient shamanism. These relationships can result in a kind of ownership, with the spirit being in a sense the property of the hunter.

Peter Geschiere emphasizes the dangerous powers held by witchcraft in Cameroon. Here, healing power has a darker side: the ability to do the opposite. Geschiere writes that some people may 'use these powers to kill' (this volume), and explains that if people are dissatisfied with their chiefs, they might turn against them and accuse them of witchcraft.

Although witchcraft in the African context is different from witchcraft in European settings, the British anthropologist Susan Greenwood discusses the biases of Western science against the notion of magical consciousness. She explains that especially in psychiatry 'such communications are often reduced to an individual's mental instability' (this volume). Greenwood herself practises Western witchcraft and is committed to spiritual healing in Britain in order to maintain individuals' physical and spiritual mental health (see also Greenwood and Doodwyn 2016).

References

Anderson, David G. 2011. "Introduction, Local Healing Landscapes." In *The Healing Landscapes of Central and Southern Siberia*, edited by David G. Anderson. Alberta: The University of Alberta Press, 1-13.

De Smet, Peter. 1999. *Herbs, Health, Healers. Africa as ethno pharmacological treasury.* Berg en Dal: Afrika Museum.

Greenwood, Susan and Erik Doodwyn. 2016. *Magical Consciousness. An Anthropological and Neurobiological Approach.* New York and London: Routledge.

Miller, Barbara. 2015. "Introduction." In *Idioms of Sámi Health and Healing*, edited by Barbara Helen Miller. Alberta: Polynya Press / University of Alberta Press, xix-xxv.

Pešoutová, Jana. 2019. *Indigenous Ancestors and Healing Landscapes. Cultural Memory and Intercultural Communication in the Dominican Republic and Cuba.* Dissertation. https://openaccess.leidenuniv.nl/handle/1887/68891

Vitebsky, Piers. 2001. *Shamanism.* Norman: University of Oklahoma Press.

Getting a second pair of eyes: the precarious balance of healing and killing in Cameroon

Peter Geschiere

For the Maka in the forest of Southeast Cameroun – as for many other groups in Africa and elsewhere – acquiring a 'second pair of eyes' is an essential threshold for getting access to the world of spirits and hidden powers. However, as my good friend Mendouga warned me – in 1971, at the beginning of my research in the area – this is a very dangerous undertaking. At the time she was the most prestigious *nganga* (healer) in the area and she mocked me for asking so many questions about the world of the witches (*mindjindjamb*). 'If you want, I can give you a "second pair of eyes". Then you can see for yourself', she said. However, the next day she had changed her mind: 'If you can see the witches, they could also see you and fall upon you'. I never knew whether she was really worried about my well-being or whether she was using irony, as she was a master in confusing people. But the message was clear: a second pair of eyes might open up exciting views, but it is also very dangerous. This ambivalence between empowerment and vulnerability is a recurrent aspect of people's imaginaries about occult forces and healing, all over the world.

Eric de Rosny, a French Jesuit priest who worked in Douala, Cameroun's main metropolis in the same forest zone and who was also initiated as a *nganga* in the 1960s, reports a similar experience, albeit much more intense, in his beautiful book about his initiation (De Rosny 1981). His first sensation after his *professeur* (teacher) had opened his second pair of eyes was that there was furious violence all around him. Only his Jesuit training, he writes, helped him to cope with the terrible fear he immediately felt. Almost at the same moment, his teacher asked for payment: '*Donne-moi.* [give to me]'. This was a second shock, as he realized at that moment that all the rumours that healers had to pay their *professeurs* 'a hairless animal' (a human being) were true. Only after tense negotiations was he allowed – as a white man – to make payment in the form of a goat, which explains the title of his book *The Eyes of My Goat*. My Maka friends who were not healers were even more precise: every healer has to pay with a relative, who is delivered into the teacher's power. Of course, healers, like my friend Mendouga, will always deny this. They insist that their initiator never asked such a thing and that, instead, he bound them with heavy interdictions to use the powers to heal, not to kill. But the Maka are never sure of this.

The power the teacher gives to (or awakens in) the apprentice healer is called '*djambe*' in Maka ('*ewusu*' in Douala). A confusing development is that Maka today translate '*djambe*' as '*sorcellerie*' (witchcraft), and the Douala do the same for '*ewusu*'. French has become current in this part of Cameroon, and this translation over time has not only greatly affected local concepts but also given new accents to the French notion. People describe the *djambe* as a small but aggressive animal (sharp teeth) that lives in a person's belly. Some know how to develop it and thus acquire the ability to transform into all sorts of animals and spirits. At night the *djambe* leave their body and fly off 'along the cobwebs of the *djambe*' to secret meetings with their mates from other villages. There the witches do horrible things. They practise what are perceived as shocking forms of sex: men with men and 'even' women with women. But the main horror is that they betray their own relatives and offer them to be 'eaten' by witches from other villages. Many elements of this imaginary will be familiar to people from elsewhere: the ability to transform oneself, the flying off in the night, the secret meetings and also the emphasis on 'witchcraft' as a threat from close by. The betrayal of intimacy (and for the Maka intimacy is mainly kinship) seems to be a general trait in such narratives (Geschiere 2013).

The forest people of South Cameroon are particularly outspoken on the moral ambiguity of these forces. There is no doubt that the *djambe* is evil: it makes the farm become infertile, stops the fire from cooking the meal and, worst of all, it makes people betray their sacred bond to their kin. Yet, the same force can be channelled to bring riches and prestige. A chief needs some degree of support in the world of the *djambe*, or he will be helpless against the jealousy of others. This ambiguity is exemplified in the figure of the healer. My friends insist that a *nganga* like Mendouga must have an overly developed *djambe*; this is why, they reason, she went to be initiated by her teacher and why she could bear the dangers of acquiring a second pair of eyes. But though they may be enjoined to use their powers for healing, healers

Figure 7 *Ngoun le Sorcier. Chaque nuit il tue les enfants qui ont un avenir meilleur* by Art Prince, Cameroon, 1996. Paint on plywood, 40 x 69,5 cm. NMVW no. TM-5723-11. Photo: Irene de Groot.

are still feared: after all, a *djambe* is a *djambe*, and one never knows when its basic instinct – to betray relatives and get them killed by witch allies – will break through. Really powerful *nganga*, it follows, should live at a safe distance from their relatives.

Across the world there are great variations in the way the balance between healing and killing is worked out. But the ambiguity seems to be widespread. In Cameroon, for instance, the Grassland societies – just outside the forest zone – have developed a much more fragmented imaginary of the occult. In these highly hierarchical societies, people insist that the chief or the healer keep a safe distance from negative uses of hidden forces. For Grassfield people, it is self-evident that their leaders must enjoy some support from the hidden world, but they are conceptually separated from those who seem to use these powers to kill. However, in everyday life such distinctions are not quite so distinct. When people become dissatisfied with their chief, they are quick to accuse him of siding with the witches. And healers are constantly tested, as well, to verify they are not 'charlatans' who connive with witches

Figure 8 *Arrestation du sorcier* by Bollo (Saturnin Wamba Djoumessi), 1990-1991. The painting shows a scene where the police uses a woman as bait to capture a man who abused his magical powers to rape and murder women in Yaoundé (Cameroon). Paint on plywood, 97 x 112 cm. NMVW no. AM-664-1. Photo: Irene de Groot.

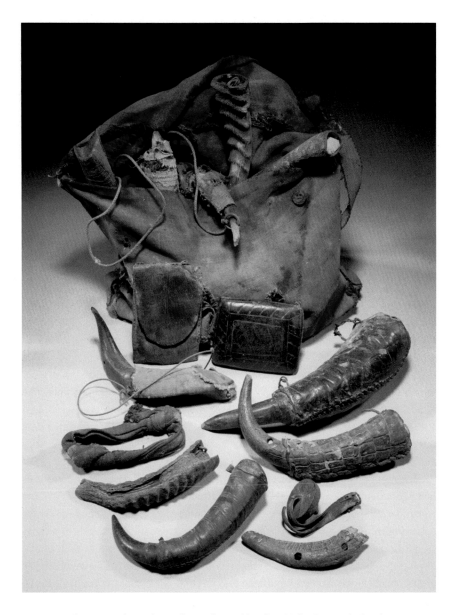

Figure 9 Bilongo medicine bag of a traditional healer. Diola, Senegal. This bag –
probably an old army bag – contains mostly animal parts. It was collected by father
H. Govers, from the Congregation of the Holy Spirit (the Spiritines, founders of
the Afrika Museum in Berg en Dal) during his work in Senegal. It belonged to an
important ritual specialist, a blacksmith and lepra doctor who was baptized. After
his death in 1965 Father Govers was able to buy the bag from the family. Normally it
would have been burned or buried with the deceased, but since he was baptized, a
bag with rubbish was placed in the grave instead. NMVW no. AM-63-38 (1 t/m 29).

instead of offering healing to their victims. Westerners should not be surprised by this resilient ambiguity. The African adage that you can only heal if you are able to kill resonates also in modern medicine. Remember that 'pharmakon' in classical Greek meant 'poison' rather than 'medicine'. This is why it was deemed necessary for doctors to take the oath of Hippocrates, to protect their patients against abuses of this special knowledge. And in the Western imaginary, the doctor remains both a healing and a frightening figure – recall all the horror stories about doctors who went astray.

In recent years, there are also great variations in the balancing of these contrasting aspects. Recent changes – especially the World Health Organization's 1978 Declaration of Alma-Ata, on primary health care for all – brought a re-evaluation of the role that could be played by local healers. In colonial times these healers had been deeply mistrusted by both missionaries and the state, and were seen as propagators of superstition and nefarious practices. But from the 1980s on, a general reorientation has occurred. In many African countries, associations of traditional healers have been created, and these are more or less formally supported by state authorities. A good example is the work of the South African Ralushai Commission, established in 1966 by the new African National Congress, almost immediately after it took over from the apartheid regime (Ralushai Commission 1996). The commission's report ends with an urgent plea to create a formal association of traditional healers in South Africa, following Zimbabwe's lead. Yet, the commission's proposal for this illustrates the ambiguities surrounding these healers, as it suggests rules to make a strict separation between bona fide healers (read: those who have traditional knowledge of healing plants) and mala fide ones (those who rather dabble in 'witchcraft' and such). The problem is that in everyday practice this separation remains untenable; this is why the commission's effort to fix it – through ever more complicated rules and formulas – reads like a somewhat pathetic attempt.

The more recent proliferation of Pentecostals and other evangelical movements in the continent has brought again another shift, since these radical Christians simply equate local healers with the Devil. Indeed, local healers are often condemned for harassing true believers after their conversion to Christianity. Evangelical pastors everywhere in the continent now regularly wage 'crusades', but, despite this dramatic display, this new offensive has not created a definitive rupture. In his vivid studies of religious dynamism on the continent, Gabonese sociologist Joseph Tonda depicts a dazzling array of new healing practitioners who combine in most imaginative ways evangelical elements with practices from local healing societies that thus become subject of a moral re-evaluation (Tonda 2002). It is probably this ambiguity of healing *and* killing, which evokes relief *and* danger, that is at the heart of the resilience of the 'traditional healer'.

References

Rosny, De E. 1981. *Les yeux de ma chèvre. Sur les pas des mares de la nuit en pays douala*. Paris: Plon. English translation: 2004. *Healers in the Night*. Eugene (OR): Wipf and Stock.

Geschiere, P. 2013. *Witchcraft, Intimacy and Trust – Africa in Comparison*. Chicago: University of Chicago Press.

Ralushai Commission. 1996. *Report on the Commission of Inquiry into Witchcraft Violence and Ritual Murders in the Northern Province*. Republic of South Africa: Ministry of Safety and Security. Northern Province.

Tonda, J. 2002. *La guérison divine en Afrique Centrale (Congo, Gabon)*. Paris: Karthala.

Intimate relations between hunters and spirits in northwest Greenland

Terto Ngiviu

The Inughuit have until recently been a shamanic hunting society. Extremely remote from the main Greenlandic population in westcoast central Greenland, the communities in the three settlements that I studied during fieldwork, in the period 2009-2014 and in 2019, still move around according to the presence of seasonal game. Whereas a decade or two ago, families would undertake very long journeys north to hunt polar bears, in recent years, the movement of whole families has decreased to only traveling to camps during the summer.

Shamans (*angakkoq*) and hunters develop a special relationship with a class of spirits called '*toornat*' (plural *-nat*, singular *-naq*). There is also a *Toornaarsuk* (a kind of super-*toornaq*), which may be either the most desired or the most frightening one to encounter. Inugguit are afraid of being close to the places that are said to be of *Toornaarsuk*.

There are both human- and animal-like spirits in the landscape, wherever you live or travel. They may manifest in sound, and only return in the form of a human or ancestral spirit if they are kept secret long enough for a person to become trustworthy enough to start a real relationship.

Inughuit explained to me that a person can be sought out by the *toornat* themselves, seeking a companion. These *toornat* are said to be in a stage of *kajungernagpagdardung*, which could be translated as 'entities wishing to be desired,

Figure 10 *Inuk woman with a polar bear* by Buuti Petersen, West Greenland, 2011. Acrylic on leather, 60 x 60 cm. NMVW no. RV-6146-5. Photo: Ben Grishaver.

seeking a person who glows with light'. The encounter may happen whilst the person is awake or asleep. At this stage, the individual having the encounter has the option to agree or not to become the 'owner' of this *toornaq*. A friend told me about his previous *aarnguaq*, a human-seal *toornaq* he encountered when he was camping on the ice in early spring with his brother. In a dream, this human-seal approached my friend and asked if he would like to acquire it. There was no language used as such, but it was a communication through the mind, and my friend understood this seal talking to him. When he agreed, this friendly human-seal disappeared and that was the end of the dream.

My friend kept the dream to himself, and he was successful more than ever, especially when it was difficult for other hunters to catch seals at all. Given that it was early summer, and the ocean was still full of fresh water from newly melted ice, which is less dense than salt water, a hunter's catch could easily sink. My friend explained that his new helper worked for him so that his seals did not sink, somehow keeping the dead seals on the surface. He was amazed at how easy it was for him to spot seals wherever he travelled. But after a few months, he became worried about being helped by this human-seal, and he revealed his relationship to someone. Once another person knew about the *toornaq*, he lost his seal-helper forever. Furthermore, my friend and his wife told me that this human-seal is known to others, has a name, and has had other owners.

Humans and those of shamanic origin depend on *anernit* (breath-spirit) to co-exist with their surroundings. There are good *anerneq* (breath spirits), suitable for those seeking a *toornaq*; these patiently wait for you, remaining quiet but gesturing to you once you've spotted them. An *anerneq* will ask if you'd like to become an 'owner' or start a relationship, and request you to touch it with your left hand. There is also an evil kind of *anerneq*, or breath spirit, that is dangerous, which you must not allow to become your *toornaq*. If this kind of *anerneq* comes towards you without stopping, you should flee from it.

Encounters with the spirit world are sometimes connected to the agency of the dead. Generally, a newborn child is named after a deceased relative. A good friend of mine, a middle-aged woman, explained that her son acquired his grandfather's name when he was around four or five, when he acted as if he remembered his grandfather's life. My friend recalled that she was scraping a sealskin on the floor of their home, with her son sitting in the chair in front of her. He suddenly started talking to her, complaining that his 'other' names had not been added to his names when he was baptised. She could see her son's eyes were very determined, and he didn't seem like her child in the way he spoke to her, but rather like her father-in-law. She knew immediately that the incident was not normal and felt she had to give her child the name of her father-in-law. This *atersortoq*, 'the name enacted', carries his old memories.

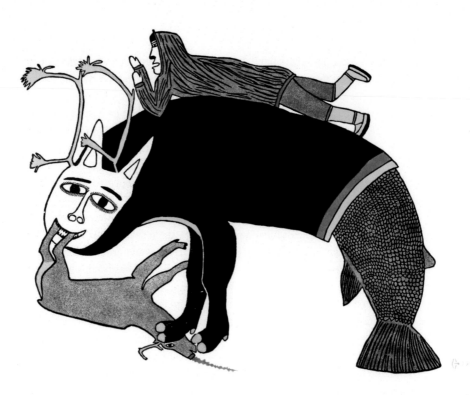

Figure 11 *Qadruhuaq, the mysterious helper* by Simon Tookoome, Qamani'tuaq (Baker Lake), 1972. A hunter is assisted by a mysterious creature, half fish, half caribou. Print, 69 × 102 cm. NMVW no. RV-6094-185. Photo: Ben Grishaver.

Another time, the child saw the pipe that had once belonged to the grandfather, and asked for tobacco and to have his pipe lit. Later on, he saw his old kayak and his hunting gear being used by another man and became angry because they were being used without his permission. This *atersortoq* then demanded to be put into his kayak and insisted that the child's dad (who was also the *atersortoq*'s son) to help him. The father was not happy about this, as the child was so small, but he felt he had to fulfil his 'father's' request. In another incident, this child was travelling in a motorboat with his parents, and asked them to go to his old settlement because he missed the place so much. I would suggest that these incidents can be interpreted as memories passed on by the dead, like a memory stick in a hard drive, which is readable until unplugged. In this case, the Name itself is both a protector of the body of the person 'possessed' and a channel to enable the dead to enter human society again (once or several times) after death.

Whilst name-spirit (*atersortoq*) can directly return to the society, helper-spirits have personhood and capabilities that are similar to the humans. Besides their particular places these helper-spirits have their personal names, and they have a common language which could be learned by ordinary humans. This language is only used in a human society when a helper-spirit has entered the shaman's body during the shaman's trance. They speak in a different tongue than the humans and have their own names, particularly of places. But in many ways, they are similar to humans: just like humans they have children, parents and ancestors, they wear the clothing of the humans around them, they hunt with the same hunting gear and sledge and dogs. They eat and give birth in the same way as humans. They also have their own shamans. And they have *toornat*, and simultaneously they themselves are *toornat* for humans. One important difference between these two groups of beings, I would suggest, is that *toornat* seek out their future owner primarily to gain human warmth, not only for company. For example, *toornat* will possess a shaman's body when they leave their body during trance. The *toornat* are a substitute for the human breath, becoming the 'breath-soul' or *anersaaq*.

When I grew up I was always being reminded that the nature around me would respond to my actions. For example, my siblings and I would often be told to finish our dinner so we could have nice weather the next day. Also, the weather on the day of one's birth mirrors their personality. *Sila* is a word for 'weather' or 'outdoor' but it also describes a person's mentality, intellectuality or consiousness. In other words, the human society of kalaallit or Inuit shares the qualities of the universe what regards outdoor conditions. *E.g.* we can say: '*silaga aalavoq*' – 'I am dizzy'. However, the direct translation is: 'my weather is moving/unstable'. The *Sila* is also an emotional and hungry entity, which can eat the flesh of humans in the cold. If your *Sila* is lost, your existence follows. If this happens, someone might ask you: '*Iluamik silannik silaqaraluarpit?*' (Are you sure you have got the right mental being? / Are you out of your mind?).

In 2013, my host mother Aminnguaq visited Nuuk, the capital of Greenland, to see a doctor, and she stayed with my sister, who lives in Nuuk. I talked with Aminnguaq by Skype the day after, and she said: "*kisianni sininga ittoorami sininneq ajuleraluarpunga*" (because my sleep [*sinik*] got shy, it took a while for me to fall asleep). I came to understand that it was not my host mother herself who had trouble falling asleep but rather her 'sleep' that had trouble falling asleep through being shy. In this way my host mother gave her *sinik* responsibility and personified it with qualities the same as a person. Furthermore, Aminnguaq was able to detach her personal senses from herself and in this way to avoid any embarrassment for her host or someone else listening to her story, who might think she was being impolite, since it was actually the 'sleep' itself that decided to be shy that night.

These are a few aspects of the spiritual culture of the Inughuit in which the landscape or 'environment' plays an important role. Everything can be inhabited by spirits, which are personified. This semi-permeability of society, and its co-existence with the 'invisible' world, also the realm of shamanism, concerns indigenous knowledge that is not necessarily shared. The contact with a *toornat* can easily be lost in case the relationship is revealed to others.

Winti healing and the Surinamese community in the Netherlands

Marian Markelo

Introduction

Winti is, according to Juliën Zaalman (2012), the philosophical and religious expression of the spiritual life that developed in Surinam during the period of slavery. In Winti, several religious strains merged, all inherited from ancestors who had been taken against their will from different parts of Africa to Surinam. From Senegal, Gambia and Liberia came the Mende, the Foula and the Sokko. The Coromantijn, the Fanti and the Delmina came from Ivory Coast and Ghana, whereas the Abo, the Papa and the Malais came from Togo and Benin (formerly Dahomey). Furthermore, the Yoruba, the Ibo and Oyo were brought to Surinam from Nigeria (Wooding 1972). Cameroon, Angola and Congo were also affected by the slave trade, and spiritual traditions from these countries also contributed to the amalgamation that became Winti. The above-mentioned regions in Africa can be distinguished into four areas that show strong similarities related to religion, language and culture (Olijfveld 2000): the Ewe Fon cultural area, the Fante-Akan area, the Mandingo and the Western-Bantu cultural area. The product of this process is Surinamese, the building blocks are African.

In Winti, believers seek wellness and harmony with the environment, the Creator and the ancestors, and the greater aim is to come into balance with the whole of existence. Winti provides its followers a structure to shape their lives, including rituals and ceremonies that help believers to experience a meaningful existence. Believers are expected to adhere to several moral codes, including abstinence (from certain food and sex), cleanliness and orderliness:

> Abstinence (*kina*). At least once a week, Winti believers reflect on our lives and morality, in terms of good and evil. We isolate ourselves in prayer and meditation, and we take a cleansing bath.

> Cleanliness. Winti believers seek to be pure and fair in our behaviour to others and be pure or clean with our body and towards the nature surrounding us. This encompasses social, physical and mental purity.

> Orderliness (*sreka*). In Winti, people are expected to maintain and take care of their relationships with their *kra*; the *kra* is the human soul, the ancestors and the Winti (powers of nature) and the Creator. The knowledge you receive and the relationships you maintain by means of rituals and ceremonies determine your behaviour.

Invisible powers and spirits

The spiritual structure of Winti encompasses the following key concepts. As just mentioned, *kra* the ancestral spirits, and the human soul is called '*akra*' or *kra*. Anana Keduaman Keduampon is the central creative power, and the powers of nature are called *yeye* or 'Winti'. These powers live in diverse realms, such as water (lakes and rivers), forest, earth and sky, and each has their characteristics and impact. These powers are not visible but they do have influence on the lives of human beings, and can create wellness and harmony; when there is disharmony between a person and the spirits, illness develops.

The concept of illness can be explained in two ways. Some illnesses can be cured by a medical doctor – educated in the biomedical science – while others can be treated by a traditional healer. This second type of illness has a metaphysical cause: one's relationship with the ancestors and the Winti can be disturbed, and this may result in physical, psychological and social disharmony. Many of those seeking out a healer feel that their Western (medical) doctor is not treating them adequately, and not providing a proper and sufficient explanation of their illness, the causes or the treatment. They may also believe their recovery needs a more holistic approach that will incorporate their soul and heart in the healing method. Winti healers give explanations about the sick person's relationship with nature and illness symptoms and experiences, and investigates their connection with the ancestors, the family-soul, the individual soul and the Winti. Healers also must treat people's psychological problems and be able to deal with positive as well as negative sides of the human mind. Not only are personal narratives, dreams, self-images and views of humanity taken into account, but also the soul is explored at its deepest layers. Sometimes a traditional healer has to teach people to accept their (Western) illness and find a creative and satisfying way to deal with it.

Healing

According to Winti healers, their practice is not folklore but a serious series of treatments, rituals and ceremonies, all performed by professionals. Healing begins with a consult in which the Winti and/or *kra* are conjured to give a clear indication of what has caused the illness. It is important to discover the history of each illness and make this visible for the help-seeker and his or her social network.

The rattle, the *agio* (cigar) and the *apinti* (drum) help healers make contact with the Winti or the *kra*. Rituals and ceremonies offer support, and dream explanations and herbs can be used. Therapeutic prayers are recited while making libations for the person in need. Ideally, the healer will experience that the inner and outer worlds are merging and see how these worlds influence each other.

Winti healers are simultaneously practical and spiritual. They are specialists in both the world of people and the world of spirits, and masters of the connections

Figure 12 Marian Markelo, winti-healer, as seen in the film interview in the exhibition *Healing Power*, 2019, Leiden. Photo: Ben Bekooy.

Figure 13 Prapi. A ceramic bowl, decorated with the snake (papa) fodu, a winti spirit, and especially used for a herbal bath for protection or healing, Surinam, 2008. 34 x 50 x 50 cm. NMVW no. TM-6395-18.

between the two worlds. Healers stay in contact with their deceased masters/ teachers, and ancestor spirits have a clear role in the healing process. In this way, Winti healers' training is life-long; their education is never completed. There is always an active transfer and exchange of knowledge, with other Winti and the ancestors or their deceased teachers.

The healer does not separate body, soul and spirit, and therefore spiritual belief and healing are part of the same process. Anana is the creative force and stands in the centre. There is not a single healing treatment that does not begin with invoking Anana, in order to steer and strengthen the human power so that the person seeking help can recover. The advantage of the Winti healer is their ability to rely on connections to the Anana and the spirits, as well as their own intuition, while a medical doctor has to work according to manuals and established protocols. Winti healers can utilize all that may help to connect to the *kra*, for example herbs and counselling. Ritual cleaning baths and specially designed objects are used. If necessary, the person seeking help may be referred to the so-called regular doctors.

Figure 14 A sick Maron woman seeks healing at an obiaman, who has put herbs in a wooden dish between them. Photographer unknown, Surinam, period 1900-1930. NMVW no. TM-60005976.

Treatment is tailored to each individual. The basis of this idea is that the energy-body of every person is different, because each person's past and recent experiences vary, as does their temperament and soul. Rituals are used to establish a connection between the personal soul of the help-seeker, the forces of nature, the ancestors and Anana. This is experienced as powerful, cleansing and healing.

Balance and harmony

Winti healing is an earthbound natural health system that balances all elements of our existence. In Winti, we believe that people, animals, plants, minerals, water, earth, fire and air are all parts of the same living earth system. Disconnections and disorder in this system cause illness in life and therefore disharmony. The healer knows inherent cohesion of the inner and outer worlds, and has the knowledge to repair breaks, through good cooperation with the spirits, emotions, family, community and nature.

References

Olijfveld, Laurens. 2000. *De mystiek van de Agida*. Lecture at De Winti Festival 4 and 5 November 2000, Den Haag.

Wooding, Charles J. 1972. *Winti, een Afro Amerikaanse godsdienst in Suriname*. Universiteit van Amsterdam. Dissertation.

Zaalman, Juliën A. 2012. *A nyame, Een uiteenzetting van de winti leer*. Paramaribo: Stichting Tata Kwasi Ku Tata Tinsensi.

Magical Consciousness and Healing Spirits

Susan Greenwood

Historically, as well as cross-culturally, the imparting of information via spirit communications – such as hearing voices or having visions – has been a central part of healing, but talking about the reality of spirits in contemporary Western cultures is often problematic. There is a systematic bias against the notion of the possibility of knowledge coming from a non-material realm in the social and human sciences, especially psychiatry where such communications are often reduced to an individual's mental instability. However, the role of spirits in therapeutic interventions is particularly relevant as it has cross-cultural implications for how we come to understand the curative procedures of cultures worldwide. The issue is how to talk about working with spirits in Western cultures heavily dominated by a materialist biomedical model, as well as a pharmaceutical industry that seeks to rationalize and dampen down such communications (Moncrieff 2008).

In this article I am going to explain my role as an anthropologist turned spirit healer by coming to negotiate a place of fusion between personal fieldwork, ethnography and theoretical exploration. Not wanting to lose my analytical thinking processes or

Figure 15 Red menstrual drum that is ridden like a horse to guide shamanic journeys, red, white and black spider rattle for creating connections in magical consciousness, and black ancestor rattle to connect with deep spirit wisdom. Photo: Susan Greenwood.

Figure 16 Part of horse rattle – my spirit guide that takes me into the realm of the dead – used in healing sessions. The shell indicates the circular notion of interconnectedness of all life and death in the right-brain hemisphere's orientation. Photo: Susan Greenwood.

my sense of a dimension that might be additional to material reality, I developed the notion of 'magical consciousness' as an alternative panpsychic aspect of perception. This does not concern any retrograde replacement of science with magic, but rather incorporates both scientific analysis and a magical knowing. Taking inspiration from Michael Polanyi (1946, 1958, 1970), who wrote that all knowing is personal and as knowers we participate within our universe, knowledge being both individual and relational, I investigated how it might be possible to entertain a subjective view that spirit communications might have a magical reality and also be therapeutic.

Overcoming Rationalism

Polanyi's view challenges dominant reductive and objective notions within the scientific community, specifically those that do not consider spirits as having reality outside of an individual's psychology, in other words the attitude that 'spirits' are 'all in the head'. But while there have been various attempts to introduce subjectivity in the sciences since the development of the empirical method in the seventeenth and eighteenth centuries, notably through phenomenology and pragmatism,[1] there is still an inherent lingering rationalism implicit in scientific attitudes. The issue is

Figure 17 One of my sacred ancestors who dwells deep in the spirit Otherworld (made by and gifted to me by shaman Gordon 'the toad' MacLellan). Photo: Susan Greenwood.

that academic and psychiatric theoretical and practical models do not allow for the possibility that spirit communications could have a reality or indeed be beneficial. By contrast, my work on magical consciousness seeks to build alternative subjective analogical patterns that accommodate more holistic experiences with spirits that fall outside of objective logical parameters.

A more holistic view is achieved through an approach to brain physiology whereby the left-brain hemisphere is more orientated toward convergent logical 'scientific' analysis, and the right-brain hemisphere has a more divergent holistic 'spirit' orientation that is non-reductive in terms of material reality. Both orientations need each other and must work together for mental health. The workings of the brain hemispheres are not discrete in terms of function as earlier lateralization theories would suggest (Gazzaniga 2002), but rather act as orientations within an intercommunicating system. The right hemisphere is more receptive to communications that are often experienced and perceived as coming from non-material dimensions.

Are these messages from a spirit receptive right-brain hemisphere orientation real or not? This question can be a red herring as it depends on your standpoint. If, as is common in biomedical science the brain is viewed as the originator of

Figure 18 Deeper into the healing issue through many levels of right-brain orientation consciousness where indications of what the problem might be lie. Insights in this realm are arrived at through intuition rather than analysis, which comes later when I return to everyday reality. Photo: Susan Greenwood.

consciousness, then spirits are not real, or only real if we believe them to be and are then manifested through placebo effects, which have their own psychological impact. However, if we look at the brain as a possible transmitter of consciousness of spirit communications, then we are open to the fact that such communications have an authenticity that might be helpful. The latter agnostic position of not considering the brain as the locus of consciousness was the one that I adopted in my research (Greenwood & Goodwyn 2016; Greenwood 2009).

I was fortunate to be able to conduct my research alongside teaching shamanic consciousness courses,[2] and over the years was gradually drawn more into the practical aspects of the work, including spirit healing. By running regular sessions whereby people were invited to have active visualizations aided by rattles and guided by the beat of a drum to induce alternate states of consciousness, I could assess the effects.

I began to see how therapeutic it could be to encourage students to develop their analogical right-brain hemisphere holistic orientations through magical consciousness. The following account comes from work done with "Lily", one of my students.

Earth Dragon Energy

My task as spirit healer was to re-orientate Lily with her own power, to reintegrate different parts of herself that she sensed were separate. In shamanic terms this is considered 'soul loss' (see Greenwood 2019). Lily agreed that her logical mind had been too dominant and that she had suppressed the magical parts, which then were revealed in dreams. She felt that her head and logical mind had been in control for so long, building a 'wall of suppression against her magical self' so that:

> [w]hen the magical gets a chance to come out to play it is like a dam bursting, because of all the pent up pressure and I have trouble controlling the rate of flow. So the head is racing to process and the gut is also racing to keep up with what is going on 'upstairs' in the mind.

Lily said that she realized that she needed to keep head and body in balance and we started working together using shamanic journeys to recover her lost parts.

During one shamanic journey Lily imagined herself within a stone circle, which she said was imbued with earth dragon energy and also represented cyclic nature, and she recorded:

The image that came to me was of a volcano (this had been a recurrent image in my mind in the last couple of days) and I knew it was symbolic of my anger [...] Wrapped around the volcano was a dragon, guarding it and spitting fire, lashing out with increasing ferocity at anyone who tried to enter the circle of the volcano.

Lily wondered what treasure the dragon was guarding, and the spirit reply was 'your harvest', meaning 'all the good experiences and things of value', which Lily interpreted as all that she had learnt or gained during the previous year.

With reference to this experience, Lily recalled another shamanic journey during which her spirit guide, a black shag sea bird, which is a bit like a cormorant, had come to her. Lily explained that this shag had commented on how much she had grown. The shag asked why she was still not accepting her anger, and why she was using it to protect herself. Lily said that she sensed that the greater the anger of the volcanic eruption within, the greater the threat to her sense of self. The spirit bird reminded her of the guidance he had previously given her to be 'ruthless in protecting my new self'. Lily replied, "How can the dragon be me?" The spirit bird just shrugged and said the dragon was 'merely a more ancient form of the bird spirit from which he was descended'. Then Lily realized slowly that the dragon was a part of her and was 'not necessarily bad'. If 'used appropriately' it could be a 'very fierce and powerful protector'. As Lily experienced this realization, the volcano calmed down and the dragon re-furled itself into the volcano's contours. In the final part of the journey the dragon was being bound by unseen forces into the rock of the volcano, which Lily now identified with herself, by thick ties 'binding us both together'.

Later I counselled Lily that at some point she would need to ride the dragon so that it did not ride her. I also suggested that the volcano image was very good and healing. This surprised Lily somewhat, but I thought that it was an indication that she was getting to the source of her emotional turmoil. I felt that her sensation of the volcano was very apt to describe her current physical, emotional and spiritual process – it represented her anger in destructive personal relationships. She needed to tread with caution and approach it slowly. At this stage of awakening, it was important to take it slowly to minimize undue trauma through the opening of strong emotions. The dragon guarding the volcano spitting fire and lashing out with ferocity seemed to be a sign that there was an enormous energy held within; this was the source of Lily's own power. My sense was that it would be helpful for Lily to be gentle with herself, not worry and try to 'ride the waves' of her changing life. It was not easy, but I sensed that it was good that Lily was getting to the volcano, underneath the 'ice and exploring the fire'. I reassured her that she would discover her place within it all, and that she would find herself stronger and more fully herself. It was a necessary part of her spiritual and emotional development, but that she should feel her way through rather than over-think.

A New Approach to World Wide Healing

Lilly's case has shown that the crucial point of understanding spirit communications is through the experience of building a strong sense of self in relation to spirit communications, rather than cutting them off as evidence of mental instability. Recognizing the value of magical consciousness and overcoming the dominance of logic in theoretical perspectives, we can see how the variances and mutual complementarity between logical and analogical modes of thought are important in maintaining individual physical and spiritual mental health. This work is part of a new approach to healing in Western cultures that recognizes several levels of reality within knowledge, and it provides a bridge of communication between Western and non-Western conceptions of worldwide spirit healing, developed in relation to the Australian Aboriginal Dreaming in further research (Greenwood 2019).

References

Moncrieff, Joanna. 2008. *The Myth of the Chemical Cure: a critique of psychiatric drug treatment*. London: Palgrave.

Polanyi, Michael. 1946. *Science, Faith, and Society*. Oxford: Oxford University Press.

Polanyi, Michael. 1958. *Personal Knowledge: Towards a Post-Critical Philosophy*. Chicago: University of Chicago Press.

Polanyi, Michael. 1970. "Transcendence and Self-transcendence." *Soundings: An Interdisciplinary Journal* 53 (1), 88-94.

Gazzaniga, Michael S. 2002. "The Split Brain Revisited". *Scientific American*: Vol. 279, no. 1 (July 1998), 50-55.

Greenwood, Susan & Erik Goodwyn. 2016. *Magical Consciousness: An Anthropological and Neurobiological Approach*. New York: Routledge.

Greenwood, Susan. 2009. *The Anthropology of Magic*. Oxford: Berg.

Greenwood, Susan. 2019. *Developing Magical Consciousness: A Theoretical and Practical Guide for Expanding Perception*. London: Routledge.

Notes

1   A discussion of phenomenology, as the early 20th century philosophical study of experience of consciousness founded by Edmund Husserl, and the work of C.S. Peirce on the pragmatism of 'semeiotic' (as opposed to 'semiotics') based on the laws of inward association are important, but outside the scope of this short article.

2   These courses started off as undergraduate modules in the School of Cultural and Community Studies at the University of Sussex instigated by psychologist Brian Bates, and then in the Continuing Education Department before I opened them to non-university students.

ZIEKTE & DISBALANS
ILLNESS & IMBALANS

"When we go into deeper layers of our consciousness, traumatic experiences, anger, sadness, fears, and what we call 'conscience' can come to the surface."

"Gezond zijn is in balans zijn, zowel fysiek, mentaal als spiritueel, op persoonlijk vlak, met de familie en met de gemeenschap."

"Being healthy means being in balance, physically, mentally, and spiritually, on a personal level, with one's family and community."

Juan-Carlos Reyes Gómez, 2015

Ritueel specialist
Ritual specialist

Een mentaal gestreste patiënt en een ex-drugs verslaafde worden gemasseerd als onderdeel van hun behandeling.
A mentally-stressed patient and an ex-drug addict are massaged as part of their treatment.

"When we go into deeper layers of our consciousness, traumatic experiences, anger, sadness, fears, and what we call 'conscience' can come to the surface."

"Gezond zijn is in balans zijn, zowel fysiek, mentaal als spiritueel, op persoonlijk vlak, met de familie en met de gemeenschap."

"Being healthy means being in balance, physically, mentally, and spiritually, on a personal level, with one's family and community." Juan Carlos Reyes Gómez, 2016

Ritual specialist.

Een mentaal gestreste patiënt en een ex-drugs verslaafde worden gemasseerd als onderdeel van hun behandeling.
A mentally-stressed patient and an ex-drug addict are massaged as part of their treatment.

ZIEKTE & DISBALANS
ILLNESS & IMBALANCE

2 Healing stories and images

Cunera Buijs and Wouter Welling

There is a great variety in the methods of healers who all have developed their own ways and means within their cultural contexts. They use various medicines, plants (spirits), hallucinogenic substances (such as mushrooms and ayahuasca), drums, priest staffs, rattles, tobacco pipes, smoke fans, and drawings. Often ritual specialists do not diagnose, as in allopathic medicine, although healers do measure the patient's pulse rate, and feel and inspect the body to find signals, which can provide information about the patient's disease or issues. The healer may concentrate on an image to solve a problem, or a revealing image may develop in the healer's psyche. Various instruments can be applied to evoke such an image. Some healers can 'read' patterns in a water bowl, while others may use tarot cards to learn about events, and in witchcraft a glass bowl provides a picture that can be interpreted (Adelaars et al 2016; Hutton 1999; Schefold 2017; Vitebski 2001, 104-105). Such visualizing methods may lead to a healing story, in connection and in communication with the client.

The Dutch biology teacher and practising witch Coby Rijkers, one of the authors of this chapter, learned about plants, herbs, animals and their healing forces from her farmer's family. She grew up in close contact with nature in the Brabantian countryside, in the south of the Netherlands. She recalls, 'Near my grandmother's chair there was always a cage with a couple of Turkish pigeons. This cured erysipelas [rash]. She made her own ointment and she performed all kinds of rituals, which I took for granted'. Traces of witchcraft practices in the Netherlands, however, are hard to find, due to four hundred years of suppression, persecution and denunciation. Rijkers therefore visited the British Museum of Witchcraft and Magic in Boscastle, Cornwall. She studied the museum's collection as well as her own Dutch roots, and

Figure 19 *Yo me lo llevo viento malo* (I ward off the evil wind) by Santiago Rodríguez Olazábal, Cuba, 1998. This installation by the Cuban regla de ifá babalawo (priest) and artist Olazábal shows a healing ritual. The babalawo (right) cleanses his patient (left) with a substance that is charged with power by the ritual objects on the beam. Among these objects is a broom that refers to Congo roots; there it is a *mpiya*, which is used by the *nganga* (the ritual specialist) to treat someone sick by warding off evil influences. The crossroads in front is a meeting point between this and the other world. Various materials, wood, textile, plastic, earth, candles and drawings in paper. 225 × 395 × 180cm. NMVW no. AM-669-2 (1 t/m 3).

developed a witchcraft school called De Wolderse Heks (the witch from Waalre). Rijkers points to the 'distance healing wax doll' as an example of image magic: parts of a person, like nails and hair, are put into a beeswax doll that is then anointed, cleansed and empowered with the elements by full moon. Next, the doll receives a name and with a straw life is blown into it. The place of the patient's illness is located in the doll. That spot is pricked with a thorn from the blackthorn plant, then the thorn is burned; with this, the illness is removed (See also Hannant and Costin 2016).

The articles in this chapter provide many illustrations of how healers may use images in their work. The drawings of Ketut Liyer, a Balinese healer, show how a healer can obtain information through an image. The ritual specialist (*balian*) in the movie *Eat Pray Love*, a 2010 biographical romantic drama, was modelled after Liyer, who draws magical figures and empowers them with a mantra; these are used to solve a problem or illness. Such drawings can be buried in the dirt floor of a house, but more often are carried on the person, explains David Stuart Fox. Several of Liyer's drawings are in the collection of the National Museum of World Cultures in Leiden.

Sigvald Persen, a healer from northern Norway, narrates another example of image magic in his joint article with Barbara Miller, 'Visions at work'. Once, a mother seeking advice concerning the court case of her adult son, called Persen. During their conversation, he had a vision, seeing a blackened, burned battlefield. Because this image persisted, Persen understood that the situation was complicated and should be dealt with carefully. The authors write that Persen considers his active holding of the initial image to be most important in his working method, which could be interpreted as active imagination.

Healing narratives and images also come to the fore in the article by the artist Daan van Kampenhout, who tells the story of spirits who protect his house while he is on vacation. One time, before he departed, he warned the spirits that there would be a friend staying in his house while he was away. However, he did not take into account that this person might invite his own guests too. An unexpected situation was the result. Van Kampenhout finds inspiration for his own artistic designs in shamans' costumes from museum collections. He translates 'images' from these old costumes, or should we rather say 'shapes' and 'compositions' or 'elements' from them, into his own creations. Shamanic parallels can be observed in his work, such as small plastic birds that evoke the water-birds often observed on nineteenth-century shamans' coats from Siberia, which enabled the shamans to fly.

References

Adelaars, Arno, Christian Rätsch, Claudia Müller Ebeling. 2016. *Rituals, Potions and Visionary Art from the Amazon*. Studio City, California: Divine Arts.

Hannant, Sara & Simon Costin. 2016. *Of Shadows: One Hundred Objects from the Museum of Witchcraft and Magic*. London: Strange Attractor Press.

Hutton, Ronald. 1999. The Triumph of the Moon: A History of Modern Pagan Witch-craft. Oxford and New York: Oxford University Press.

Schefold, Reimar. 2017. *Toys for the Souls. Life and Art on the Mentawai Islands*. Bornival: Primedia sprl.

Vitebsky, Piers. 2001. *Shamanism*. Norman: University of Oklahoma Press.

A Dutch way to witchcraft: the 'Wolderse Heks' from Waalre

Coby Rijkers

I grew up amidst completely self-sufficient and respectably aged, wise family members. On Saturdays we baked bread and churned goat milk, and we lived the entire year from the products of our vegetable garden, our orchard, and our sheep, whose mutton we canned. The toilet was outside; there was no tap water. I slept alone in the attic, where canaries and other birds made love and provided an extra source of income.

The attic was divided by a heavy curtain that hung from the ceiling, creating a world of light before the curtain and an obscure, dark world behind it. In autumn, behind my bed, the star apples were stored and spread their recognizable sloppy sweet smell. In the dark world, the potato harvest was stocked, covered against the frost with a good layer of old ancestor coats, which came to life in my fantasies at night. It was a magical, inhospitable corner, where scary ghosts danced and at the same time the place of the family's night-time chamber pot.

I was brought up with love for and connection to nature by three generations. Surrounded by countless animals, high trees and an over-concerned family clan, I entered school at the age of five, having been totally estranged from the larger human world. Every day, coming home, I felt the relief that I could embrace in all solitude and silence my favourite toy, a dead mole. I was well connected: my great uncle was a mole catcher.

The mystery of death has always appealed to me, and my early work as an obstetrician's assistant resulted in my first encounter with a ghost. That acquaintance with the other side had quite an impact. I had long conversations about it with a co-worker, a pathologist-anatomist and Jesuit from South Yemen. He was an expert in the field of ghost appearances and told me that people who were suddenly pulled out of life often appeared in the world of the living. My fear of ghosts changed into curiosity. After I completed my degree in biology, my partner George took the children and me on a holiday to Cornwall, England. In Boscastle we visited the 'Museum of Witchcraft' for the first time. It was there that my fascination with traditional witchcraft began.

Now, almost seventeen years later, I browse through the by now more than 2,000 pages of the textbook I wrote for the students enrolled in our traditional witchcraft school. And after all those years I have that 'attic feeling' once again. Three days a week I'm standing in front of a class in the light and busy world, while the rest of the time I wrap myself in the energy from times long gone, in the place where I grew up, among trees now old, surrounded by owls, ravens, cats and a legion of other animals. In this dark and magic space, I cherish the buttons on my ancestors' coats, and I pass

Figure 20 Coby Rijkers at her home, holding one of her owls. Taken from the film interview in the exhibition *Healing Power*, Leiden 2019. Photo: Ben Bekooy.

on the gathered ancient knowledge to our students, sitting in the dark by the light of a flickering candle.

My many years of searching delivered, and still deliver, insight into many forgotten oracle techniques, old recipes and magical rituals, the timing of which was connected to the phases of the moon. Traditional witchcraft mainly dealt with innumerable ways of healing and protecting against evil. 'Witch bottles' were amply filled with morning urine and equipped with forceful weapons like rusty nails and sharp thorns. Then the stuff was activated with the famous 'Witches' Ladder', a red thread with nine knots in which the purpose was locked with the aid of a magic spell. Sealed, the bottle was hidden under the floor, from where it protected the witch. If the bottle was found and ended up in a fire, the witch's life was in peril. The 'Witches' Ladder' was also used to attract things or to cure. In order to send the wish into the universe and strengthen it, feathers or bones were knotted into it. Every witch had her own kind of magic. Many wise women began their careers with a practice at home, as folk healers or midwives, and mostly sold spells against curses. Consulting rooms were decorated with terrifying objects such as skulls, mirrors and dried animal parts to impress clients. Poisonous mixtures of herbs were carried in pouches in order to reverse curses, and their efficacy would have to be extended on a regular basis as the moneybag had to remain filled. The most famous preparation was the fly ointment, an extremely poisonous substance with hallucinogenic qualities. The mandrake root, whose shape is similar to the human form, was thought to have secret forces. Soaked in wine it worked as a narcotic; worn as an amulet it provided great power in the fight against sickness and suffering.

Small bags filled with sand taken from a three-way intersection, teeth and bones from an old graveyard were used as a powerful tool (graveyard dust) against curses and diseases. Because these things had passed through all the gates of alchemy, they were considered to be very forceful. The SATOR square, a magical square, was applied as a strong weapon against many kinds of evil. The ABRACADABRA triangle, worn around the neck, protected against the plague and drove away high fever. Contagious magic, such as selling warts and other miseries, was often implemented. A remnant of this activity can be seen in the children's game of tag, in which one eagerly passes on one's energy to another. A glass bottle in green, a healing colour, stuffed with hair and nails from a sick person, supplemented with herbs and magical elements, was often used as a 'healing bottle' to chase away all kinds of terrible diseases.

Distance healing often offered relief. A doll was made of beeswax and given the name of the diseased; life was blown into it, and when the spot where the afflicted person felt pain was pricked with a sharp thorn during the full moon, the disease vanished. Old, worn socks were loaded with herbs and other things; thus transformed into a 'witch doll', they were used to cure sleeping disorders.

The traditional witch created healing ointments. The base was mainly pork fat, and the Band-Aid was a piece of dried pork bladder or Judas's ear, a mushroom that can often be found on an old elderberry tree. At my grandma's place, after the slaughter, there was always an old preserving jar ready for the rendered fat: warmed on a saucer on the woodstove till well above body temperature, it could be used to anoint all kinds of injuries or for a common cold. The warm fat was covered with a flannel cloth, and in the morning you could reapply it again. At least that's what was expected of you. Pork fat has a tremendous depth effect, penetrates deep into the skin layers and muscles, and herbs can easily be brewed in it. With it, one can make nettle ointment, comfrey root ointment or Balm of Gilead, a delicious smelling balm of the beneficial resin of poplar buds. In this context the Spagyrian life elixir should also be mentioned. For each day of the week, a tincture was made, brewed from a plant that corresponded to the day of intake and related celestial body. Everything was prepared according to the seven gates of Alchemy, involving seven consecutive chemical procedures in which the plant is dissected and later on in the light of the full moon reunited, in an operation called *marriage*. Daily consumption of this magical elixir ensures the user of a long and healthy life. Preparation of the Spagyrian life elixir takes at least a year. For decades the bark of the willow has provided people

Figure 21 Mandrake. Photo: Ben Bekooy.

Figure 22 Overview of the showcase of Coby Rijkers in the Healing Power exhibition. Photo: Ben Bekooy.

relief from pain and fever. After consumption, the salicin in the bark is transformed in the intestine into salycil-alcohol, out of which the liver makes salycilic acid; this active ingredient, originated by the collaboration of man and plant, has been mass-produced under the name of aspirin since 1900. And of course within the theme of healing we should not forget soap. It was discovered at the foot of a sacrificial place where fat and ashes united, and its disinfecting effect resulted in a drastic reduction of the number of fatal infections.

Over the centuries, the image of the witch has not changed: she wears a tall, black, pointed hat and a black cape, and flies on a broom or a fork, the 'witches stang'. The origin of the pointed hat is still a mystery, but a hat in this form was fashionable around 1700. The broom is but a cleaning tool, but it was also used by women in the countryside to expel old energy from the fields before sowing. In the light of the full moon the witch took the broom between her legs and jumped in the air to indicate how high the grain should grow. This old fertility ritual resulted in the image of the flying witch. The traditional witch was and is not religious, whereas Wicca, the new witchcraft that started in the 1950s, is. Luckily, centuries of persecution against witches have not resulted in the loss of their knowledge; together with my partner, I pass on this knowledge with great enthusiasm.

Visions at work: when an untold story becomes a ghost

Barbara Helen Miller and Sigvald Persen

Sigvald Persen is a Sámi healer living in northern Norway.[1] He works together with Barbara Helen Miller, anthropologist and Jungian psychoanalyst. Sigvald introduced himself with these words at the Expert Meeting on World Wide Healing on 1-2 May 2017, in Leiden:

> I experience in my North Norway environment that it is not safe to be outspokenly Sámi, which has to do with the long history of Norwegianization. From my parents I learned values that contain an understanding for spiritual life, however, today in my local Sámi community there appears to be no ongoing interest, that is, locally, I am not asked to share ancestral values. Here today at this gathering I am not burdened with Norwegianization and there has been shown an interest in my ancestral values. Hence, I can speak freely, and share with you something of my praxis. Firstly, how I am approached: often my first contact with a person seeking help is from being telephoned. During the time that the individual speaks to me about their story, an image can appear. This vision, which I assume has some relationship with their story – their talk about what is happening – is first just held by me. I hold a question concerning whether any change will occur in the image. There is work involved for the change in the image to happen, which is the work with this vision. For example, I had a horse that after being loaned out returned with a large saddle sore. Much effort had already been made by veterinarians to heal this wound, but without effect. I considered putting the horse down, but before this, held the image of the open wound in my mind. I was checking to see if it would be possible to move or change things. Because the image *did* change, indeed, moving towards the wound becoming smaller and smaller, it seemed to me that the healing of this wound would be possible. I applied a natural healing salve made of bird cherry bark and things started to happen differently. The wound became smaller and smaller, and it healed totally with new hair covering it. (. . .) The help that people may feel they receive through consulting me is not *my* achievement. I will never claim to have healed or to have helped. It is the spiritual connection that does the work.

In this article, we elaborate on this excerpt from Sigvald's speech.

Shamanism was an ingredient of pre-Christian Sámi culture and the pre-Christian 'old' religion, which had a pronounced bear ceremonialism. The religion included sacrifices to the life-giving powers, held at special locations called in Sámi '*sieidi*'. Sámi religion was woven into everyday social conduct, where certain codes of respect toward *sieidi* were important. The pre-Christian Sámi term for the Sámi healer is '*noaidi*', and scholars have concluded that this occupation had diverse social roles similar to the shaman (Bäckman and Huktkrantz 1978). While there are many similarities, there are also differences between Sámi shamanism and the shamanism of other regions. For example, the Sámi shaman differed from the Siberian shaman in the lack of any special attire. Also the initiation period did not contain an experience of dying and dismemberment, and *noaidi* did not use the central world tree/pillar as a channel of communication with, or transportation to, the beyond. The Sámi shaman did, however, employ the drum and enlist spirit helpers (Hultkrantz 1992).

The category of shamanism does not exist in a unitary form, and current scholars speak of a plurality of 'shamanisms', each embedded in particular worldviews as well as in wider systems of thought and practice (Atkinson 1992). A minimal definition is that to shamanize is 'to come into contact with the world of the gods and spirits through certain preparations' (Bäckman and Huktkrantz 1978, 69). In northern Norway, these 'certain preparations' may have included drumming. Drums were confiscated and forbidden during the seventeenth century in Sweden and eighteenth century in Norway. The missionaries saw the use of the drum exclusively in connection with *noaidi* praxis, but drumming was also used for orientation, as an oracle, as guidance to know where and when to hunt, fish, sacrifice, etc., by several members of the community (Scheffer 1704, 149). Today, Sámi traditional healers work without drums, and most often consider themselves to be Christian. The healer is no longer referred to as '*noaidi*', or by the cross-cultural term 'shaman', but by other terms, such as 'improver', 'one who returns', 'one who knows' and 'reader.' However, the Sámi healer is still an inspirational healer.

Focusing on the Sámi healer as an inspirational healer can help us view the possible line of inheritance. During pre-Christian practice, the 'healer' beat the drum and 'travelled', so it was said, using the small images painted on the drum's skin: skies, boats, birds, whales, fish and reindeer. The prohibition of the drum, however, did not stop the practice of travelling through images. For example, a person could remove his/her belt, hang it on the wall, address it (as in prayer) and visions were facilitated. The belt had symbolic significance because it 'bundled' the outer garment and when addressed will 'bundle' the thoughts. In the late nineteenth and early twentieth century, a local Christian practice called Laestadianism also encouraged visions. Lars Levi Laestadius (1800-1861), a Lutheran minister in northern Sweden, led a religious movement within the Lutheran Church with pietistic roots[2] (Outakoski 1987, 208-210; Steen 1954; Zorgdrager 1989).

Here, we highlight the similarity between the Sámi healer employing the helping spirit (*noaidegaccit*) for visions and the pietistic practice of employing the Christian Holy Spirit for visions. The pietistic understanding is that knowledge is acquired through visions instigated by the Holy Spirit (Brown 1996). The Holy Spirit can

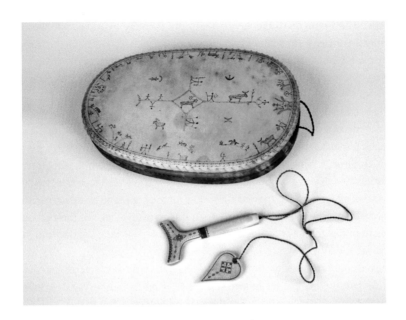

Figure 23 Sámi drum by A. Sunna, Tärnaby, Sweden, 1976. Animal skin, wood, reindeer antler. NMVW no. RV-6072-20. Photo: Irene de Groot.

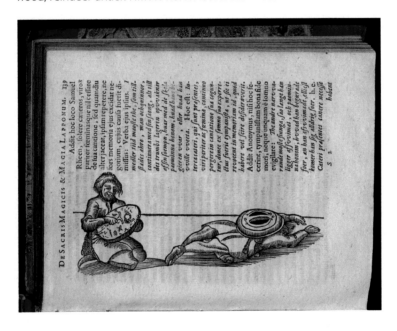

Figure 24 Sámi *noaidi* with his drum and subsequently in trance, as illustrated in Johannes Schefferus's Lapponia, 1673, Frankfurt, Christian Wolff, page 139.[3] Courtesy University Library Leiden.

enter one who reads the Bible, giving them the capacity to go beyond the Bible's theoretical knowledge to its living knowledge (Matthias 2005). Both the discourse in Christianity and that in shamanism circle around the 'entry of the spirit': While shamanic discourse is concerned with how, when and where a shaman received the 'helping spirit', Christian/Laestadian discourse repeats, that is, *passes on* the story of how Christians received the Keys to Heaven.

In several interviews with local Laestadians, Barbara Miller (2007, 69) was told that Jesus Christ left the Keys of Heaven to Peter, and through Peter to the early Church. In these interviews, Laestadians quoted the Bible for emphasis: 'And when he said this he breathed on them, and saith unto them, Receive ye the Holy Ghost. Who soever sins ye remit, they are remitted unto them; and who soever sins ye retain, they are retained' (John 20:22-23). In this narrative, we see the regenerated congregation has the Keys to Heaven, and with these, the congregation can bundle and release sin.

Nanna, the Sámi healer Barbara interviewed, who is an active member of the local Laestadian Congregation and also Sigvald's mother, called herself a 'Christian helper' (not 'healer'). She described healers as inheriting 'the gift that can be given', which resonates with the gifting of the Keys to Heaven. Important to note is that with the 'helping spirit' one also inherits its history. Nanna explained that she had received the gift from a former Sámi healer. Without being explicit, she conveyed her understanding that the 'gifted' use of binding and releasing forms the correct connection with the Christian God, and, she shared the local Laestadian pastor's view: 'the Keys have always been among God's children' (Miller 2007, 69). In this understanding the Sámi were Christian even before the missionaries came to Christianize them, hence locals did not demonize Sámi healing practice. The gifted one can 'see' the wrong connections, and make the correct connections.

Among the Sámi, the understanding is that for a child to be well, it needs to receive a name, and that wellbeing is when life is peaceful. Disruptions and accidents are indications of possible incomplete or incorrect connections; baptism forms an important connection, establishing a complete social identity. Local communities (occasionally) have some sense that a newborn infant has been born that the mother has abandoned in an out of the way place. Such a nameless dead infant is called an '*eahpáraš*'. With its social identity unestablished, an *eahpáraš* stays with what it knows, the location of its death, which it haunts. Such a location evokes the experience of having no peace, and people who pass near to it will hear the *eahpáraš*'s complaints. A healer will go to the location and talk to the *eahpáraš*, and say, 'It is now known what has happened'. When the story gets told, the connection to God is made, the haunting of the location is lifted, and there is peace at this location. The healer who has the gift can form the final connection for what was haunting and thereby solve the problem.

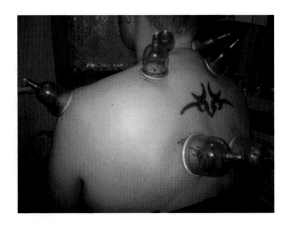

Figure 25 Cupping by
Sigvald Persen.

There is a close resemblance between the Christian Keys to Heaven and
Sámi healing. With the receiving of the Keys, the Holy Ghost brings visions (as at
Pentecost). The Keys are implements for binding and unbinding, and are used to form
connections that God sanctions so that sins may be forgiven. Similarly, when the gift
of healing is passed from a healer to their successor, visions become available; the
gift facilitates the holding of visions that bundle thoughts, and can release the ghost
by bringing untold parts *into* the story.

Sigvald promised to care for his mother's gift. Here he shares with us the
healing process:

> An elderly woman called and told me about her pain. She said it was kidney
> stones. When talking, I see a vision of the whole thing, and I start to work with
> it. After the call I continue, [and] I see that the vision changes, I see that the
> stones are crushed and are released. A day or so later she calls and tells that
> it is now all in order, she has no more pain. Also letting me know that she had
> done nothing more than make this call to me. Frequently, I simply say, 'Let us
> bundle our thoughts'. The patient has a sense that there comes something out of
> it. When two people 'hold', something gets made.

References
Atkinson, J.M. 1992. "Shamanisms Today." *Annual Review of Anthropology* 21, 307-330.
Bäckman, L., and Å. Huktkrantz. 1978. *Studies in Lapp Shamanism*. Stockholm:
    Almqvist and Wiksell.
Brown, D.W. 1996. *Understanding Pietism*. Nappanee: Evangel Publishing House.
Eidheim, H. 1971. *Aspects of the Lappish Minority Situation*. Tromsø:
    Universitetsforlaget.

Hætta, O.M. 1996. *The Sami, an Indigenous People of the Artic*. Karasjok: Davvi Girji.

Hansen, L.I. and B. Olsen. 2004. *Samenes historie fram til 1750*. Oslo: Cappelen Akademiske Forlag.

Hultkrantz, Å. 1992. "Aspects of Saami (Lapp) Shamanism." In: *Northern Religions and Shamanism* edited by M. Hoppál and J. Pentikäinen, 138-145. Helsinki: The Regional Conference of the International Association of the History of Religions: Finnish Literature Society.

Matthias, M. 2005. "August Hermann Francke (1663-1727)." In: *The Pietist Theologians* edited by C. Lindberg, 100-114. Malden, MA: Blackwell Publishing.

Miller, B. H. 2007. *Connecting and Correcting, A Case Study of Sámi Healers in Porsanger*, 69. Leiden: CNWS.

Outakoski, N. 1987. "Cuorvvot." In: *Saami Religion*, edited by T. Ahlbäck, 208-210. Åbo: The Donner Institute for Research in Religious and Cultural History.

Scheffer, J. 1704. *The History of Lapland*. (Translated from the 1673 edition in Latin), 149. London: Parker under the Royal Exchange.

Steen, A. 1954. *Samenes Kristning og Finnemisjonen til 1888*. Oslo: Avhandlinger utgift av Egede Instituttet 5.

Vorren, Ø. and E. Manker. 1962. *Lapp Life and Customs*. London: Oxford University Press.

Zorgdrager, N. 1989. *De Strijd der Rechtvaardigen. Kautokeino 1852*. Utrecht: Proefschrift University Utrecht.

Notes

1   The Sámi are the indigenous people of northernmost Europe. Many Sámi communities historically practised a semi-nomadic lifestyle. It was not uncommon to combine reindeer herding with hunting, fishing and farming, or to combine fishing with small-scale farming (Hætta 1996, 20). The Sámi in Norway were Christianized mostly during the early eighteenth century (A. Steen 1954; Hansen and Olsen 2004). Today the Sámi are a minority group within Norway, Sweden, Finland and Russia, where they number approximately 70,000. They are predominantly engaged in a variety of modern occupations (Eidheim 1971; Vorren and Manker 1962).

2   Pietism is a Lutheran movement that originated in seventeenth-century Germany that stressed personal piety over religious formality and orthodoxy.

3   In this publication, Schefferus quotes Isaac Olsen, here translated into English: 'He faints and seems to be dead and his face becomes black and blue (...) and he can become normal again, and when he is in such a state, he can have knowledge and can narrate extensively and without end about many things, when he wakes up, which he has been seeing or has been done, and he knows about countries and many places in different times and he uses certain signs and he can acknowledge things, when he is asked for it and he goes into a fight with his protagonists in another world, until the person [he is treating] is alive again and cured from his wounds.'

Drawings in Balinese Healing and Magic

David J. Stuart-Fox

Modern Western-style health care in Bali has not replaced all of the traditional medical practice that Bali's healers provided to their communities. Still today, healers treat physical and psychological illnesses as well as ailments associated with magic and sorcery. The healer is a respected member of his (or, occasionally, her) community, and once every Balinese year of 210 days, patients offer gratitude through worship of the healer's divine patron, the goddess Saraswati. At the same time, there prevails a certain anxiety or distrust, even fear, as the healer works within a world of spiritual and supernatural powers that for Balinese are by no means always auspicious.

Less often than in times past but still quite frequently, villages in Bali have one or more healers (*balian*) providing services corresponding to their specialty. There can be a *balian usada*, a healer practising within the written tradition (*usada* refers to texts dealing with disease and healing); a *balian katakson* who through trance makes contact with the other world and so can provide advice for treating various ailments; a specialist bone-setter or masseur; someone who through the usually 'miraculous' discovery of an object of power, often for just a limited period is able to treat a variety of complaints. Modern health care cannot, however, handle cases of sorcery which is still a widely accepted fact of life. Because the healer works within the supernatural world, his means of treatment, besides herbal medicines, include aspects such as holy water and mantras that belong to priestly practice. One of those therapeutic means used by the *balian usada* are special drawings of power.

Ketut Liyer, a *balian usada* from the village of Pengosekan, near Ubud, and the healer made famous by the book and film *Eat Pray Love*, is an expert in these drawings. When I first knew Ketut Liyer, he showed me an old exercise book full of extraordinary drawings, strange, quite unlike anything I had then seen.[1] He utilized these drawings in his healing practice. Balinese call them *rerajahan*, a term for drawings with a potential 'supernatural' (*niskala*) power or agency adopted in certain rituals, especially those associated with healing and 'magic'. Balinese believe strongly in the existence of the *niskala* world of deities, spirits and unseen powers. The word *niskala*, used always in relation to *sakala*, is difficult to gloss, but briefly, *sakala* refers to whatever is knowable by the senses, *niskala* to whatever is not knowable by the senses. Although the term *rerajahan* is generally related to healing and sorcery, the active form of the word, *ngrajah*, means to write or inscribe drawings, formulas, and letters of the Balinese alphabet on instruments used in ritual contexts, ranging from temple ceremonies to sorcery. The materials of these instruments include cloth, paper, bark paper, *lontar* leaf, metal foils, rice flour,

leaves, and the human body. Certain kinds of drawings form separate categories (*e.g. kajang* in cremation rites, and *ulap-ulap* for the 'animation' of buildings).

Like many of his fellow healers, Liyer borrowed texts from colleagues and copied them. Especially since the 1920s and 1930s, when pens and paper and exercise books became common, drawings and texts on healing and magic were often copied into such books. It was a lot easier than drawing onto the prepared leaves of the *lontar* palm, the original writing material in Bali. Indeed, it takes a skilled hand using a special knife to scratch drawings onto *lontar* leaf.[2]

A small number of *rerajahan* manuscripts entered museum collections. Whether on *lontar* leaf or on paper, their artistic qualities vary considerably. But certainly, one masterpiece among *rerajahan* collections is a paper 'manuscript' of loose sheets in the National Museum of World Cultures in Leiden.[3] Nothing is known about this work other than it was sold to the museum by the Swiss painter Willy Quidort (1898-1978) in 1975.[4] The accompanying customs document describes it as "120 Seiten gezeichnete Kopien eines balinesischen Medizinbuches" (120 sheets of drawn copies from a Balinese medicine book). Whether the drawings were copied from an original paper manuscript or direct from *lontar* books is unknown. The drawings are beautifully done, in black ink with touches of red in many places, on loose sheets of good quality paper. They are in mint condition, seemingly never used. It is very likely that Quidort commissioned them during his stay in Bali. The painter is unknown.[5]

Rerajahan drawings were normally part of a larger text; there is no 'complete' or 'standard' collection. Some *lontar* books have just a few images, others quite a large number. Collections are also available in Balinese publications. In essence, *rerajahan* are independent items. From the *rerajahan* that he has in his library of books and *lontars*, the healer chooses the one or several that he needs for a particular patient or purpose. A *rerajahan* is accompanied by a text which generally gives the name of the drawing, its purpose, and how it is to be utilized. Occasionally special mantras or offerings are prescribed; otherwise the healer uses a general

Figure 26 The upper drawing of the upside-down demon Sungsang Kala is an amulet to protect a house (*tumbal umah*); it must be hung up above the doorway. The bottom-left drawing called Essence (Sari) of Mpu Bhawula, is 'protector of the soul' (*pangraksa jiwa*), thus of life itself. Very superior since it is the gift of the deity Sanghyang Mrajapati, anyone using this formula/drawing (*aji*) will not be punished or defeated by a 'person of power' (*manusa sakti*), suggesting that the drawing may be used as protection against sorcery. The drawing can be placed in a sash or carried (as an amulet). The third nameless drawing is likewise a 'protector of the soul' (it is a common purpose) and 'remover of the efficacy of an object of sorcery' (*pamunah papasangan*); the mantra calls on the deity 'Reverser of Desti', *desti* being a form of sorcery. Bali, probably 1935-1945, ink on paper, 34 x 21,5 cm. NMVW no. RV-4844-16; Hooykaas 1980a illustration no. 53, 196-197. Photo: Irene de Groot.

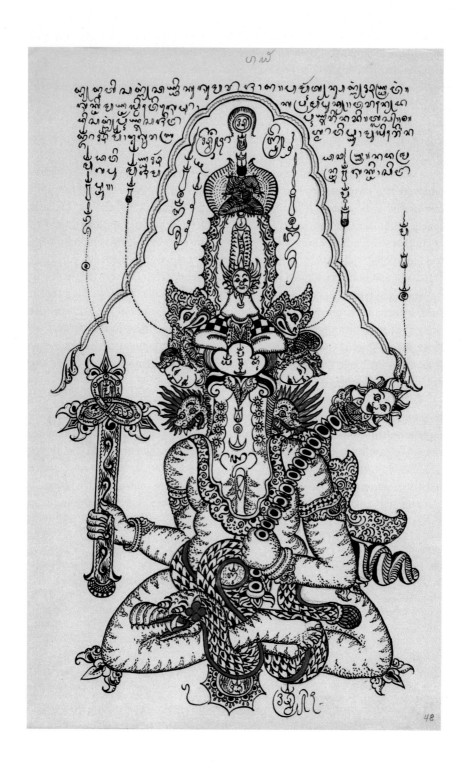

mantra to empower the drawing. This instils agency into the drawing so that it can go about its work, whenever necessary.

From the hundreds of different drawings in Balinese texts – one might ask why so many – the actions that drawings (and mantras) can perform are extremely varied.[6] It is possible to divide these into broad categories, such as those of protection or defence and those of attack. These categories are not quite the same as the distinction made between 'magic' of the right (*panengen*) and 'magic' of the left (*pangiwa*), the latter being comparable to sorcery or 'black magic' (an English expression not uncommon now on Bali). The relationship between categories and ethics is complex. Many drawings are ethically neutral, others are ambivalent; how they are used determines a person's judgment of them. And this is especially so with regard to sorcery, where rivalry or battle between healer and sorcerer or between sorcerers is a common idiom. A drawing of protection can be used by a healer against a sorcerer's magic or by a sorcerer against a healer's or another sorcerer's actions.

Accompanying texts frequently associate such actions with a particular kind (or kinds) of ailment or condition. A healer such as Ketut Liyer works with complex multiple etiologies of illness, often in combination, whose treatments likewise involve various methods. With the exception of purely physical or dietary problems and certain kinds of poisoning, curable with traditional medicines, causes are regarded as *niskala* (spiritual or supernatural) in nature or involve intervention by *niskala* beings or powers. A healer might treat symptoms, but he must also address the *niskala* origins. Formerly untreatable illnesses such as plague or cholera were considered as having *niskala* roots. Many conditions, especially those with a psychological dimension, are believed to be caused by human actors, particularly sorcery. Neglect of *niskala* beings such as gods, demons, ancestors and birth-siblings (*kanda mpat*),[7] mistakes in ritual practice, problems arising from placement of buildings, or from date of birth according to complex calendrical and divinatory systems, can all result in ailments.

Once a healer such as Ketut Liyer has determined the nature of the illness or complaint and its probable origin(s), he must first decide whether a *rerajahan* drawing is suitable. If it is, he chooses the drawing based on its indicated powers, and in many cases on the encompassment of the drawing's powers, for he is often

Figure 27 This highly complex drawing is called Sanghyang Candi Kusumaraja, a wrathful form (*pamurtian*) of Sanghyang Andhrawang. In Balinese iconography the wrathful form is indicated by multiple bodies, here three diminishing in size one above the other, and by multiple heads. The drawing is said to be very powerful. The purpose of the drawing and its method of use is not indicated; the practitioner would decide for himself. Bali, probably 1935-1945, ink on paper, 34 x 21,5 cm. NMVW no. RV-4844-48; Hooykaas 1980a illustration no. 227. Photo: Irene de Groot.

uncertain of the nature of the *niskala* power generating the ailment. It may also be based on the name of the drawing, for a drawing named after or associated with a major deity is thought to have special power. Moreover, it is founded on long experience as well.

Accompanying texts generally indicate where the drawing is to be placed. It may be on top of a door (see Figure 26), buried in the grounds of the house, in the fields, by the bathing place or by the water pot. More often though it is to be carried on the person. If just a single drawing, it is normally wrapped in a piece of white cloth and either sewn into clothing or carried in some other way. Often though, the texts frequently prescribe that the drawing or more often several drawings be placed in a waist sash usually made from white cotton fabric (*sabuk*). Ketut Liyer often fashioned sashes for his clients, sometimes as a cure for a diagnosed ailment but also as an instrument of general protection, especially against sorcery.

Then follows the ritual of empowerment. Like a temple priest, a *balian* must undergo the rite of *mawinten* before beginning his practice, which has much in common with that of the priest. The *balian*, through the medium of water and fire (incense), offerings and mantra, makes two kinds of holy water, one for removing impurities (*tirta panglukatan*) and one for purification and blessing (*tirta pabresihan*). These two processes are central to Balinese ritual. To empower the drawing or sash, the *balian* sprinkles first the *panglukatan* and then the *pabresihan*. Only then will he utter the mantra(s) of empowerment, the bestowal of agency or life or power, all are possible glosses of the rite of *masupatinin*. The amulet is ready for use. To retain its efficacy, the client must look after it. He must provide offerings on certain holy days and sprinkle it with holy water.

Figure 28 This superb drawing Geni Salambang portrays an immense coiling *naga* serpent whose head is in the form of a three-headed demonic figure, as if the serpent tale emerges from its midriff. Fire issues from all over body and tail, hence its name meaning perhaps something like 'Fire portrayed'. It is said to be a 'cover of the world' (*panangkeb jagat*), suggesting protection; but also a *pangrong*, in the translation of Christiaan Hooykaas (1980b, 207) a way 'to rob (an enemy of invulnerability)', 'to avert (bullets)', or 'a means to acquire control (of another's body)'; or 'a means to capture something or someone' (*pangjukan*). Its potential for either sorcery or its eradication is indicated by the accompanying mantra: "ONG, ... your legs are unable to walk, your hands are unable to hold, for I am Fire Portrayed, Fire of the World. Your ears are unable to hear, your mouth is unable to talk, your nose is unable to smell." It is to be used in a sash, as 'protector of life', drawn on yellow silk. Bali, probably 1935-1945, ink on paper, 34 x 21,5 cm. NMVW no. RV-4844-113; Hooykaas 1980a illustration no. 315. Photo: Irene de Groot.

　　　　HEALING POWER

References

Hooykaas, C. 1980a. *Tovenarij op Bali: magische tekeningen uit twee Leidse collecties.* Amsterdam: Meulenhoff.

Hooykaas, C. 1980b. *Drawings of Balinese sorcery.* Leiden: Brill.

Rhodius, Hans. [1964]. *Walter Spies: Schönheit und Reichtum des Lebens (Maler und Musiker auf Bali 1895-1942).* Den Haag: Boucher.

Stuart-Fox, David J. with Ketut Liyer. 2015. *Pray, magic, heal: the story of Bali's famous* Eat, pray, love *folk healer.* New York & Leiderdorp: New Saraswati Press.

Notes

1   The story of Ketut Liyer, with a selection of drawings commissioned for the book, is told in David J. Stuart-Fox with Ketut Liyer, *Pray, magic, heal: the story of Bali's famous* Eat, pray, love *folk healer* (New York & Leiderdorp: New Saraswati Press, 2015).

2   A related art form is the *prasi*, lontar books of multiple leaves telling a story, usually with accompanying text, rather like a comic book; they are still being made for the tourist market.

3   This manuscript (RV-4844) was published by C. Hooykaas in his book *Tovenarij op Bali: magische tekeningen uit twee Leidse collecties* (Amsterdam: Meulenhoff, 1980), together with a shorter manuscript from the Korn collection (KITLV/Leiden University Library collection). Surprisingly, Hooykaas did not follow the original manuscript page by page, but re-ordered the drawings without any apparent logic, numbering them 1 to 320. In a couple of cases, two parts of a single drawing were counted separately. And occasionally he rearranged the accompanying text, or left a section out (e.g. plates 3 and 4 of this article). Furthermore the black-and-white reproductions do not reflect the fine quality of the original drawings, nor the highlighting in red of details in many of them.

4   Willy Quidort travelled to Bali in 1937 or 1938, together with another Swiss painter Ernst Albert Christen (1914-1988). He settled in Ubud and built a house at Campuan, near the home of Walter Spies who befriended him. Spies appreciated Quidort's knowledge of technical aspects of painting and preparation of canvases. See Hans Rhodius, *Walter Spies: Schonheit und Reichtum des Lebens (Maler und Musiker auf Bali 1895-1942)* (Den Haag: Boucher, [1964]). According to Georges Breguet (to whom many thanks), he was said to be rich and did not need to make a living from his art.

5   It might possibly be the work of I Dewa Ketut Ding of Padangtegal, near Ubud. Reproductions of palm-leaf *prasi* drawings by I Dewa Ketut Ding (1912-1996) illustrate an article by Quidort in the magazine *Minjak* (Bali-nummer, October-November 1941); other articles and photographs by Quidort, and black-and-white reproductions of his paintings are found in the same magazine.

6   C. Hooykaas, *Drawings of Balinese sorcery* (Leiden: Brill, 1980), p. 203-209 provides a list of more than 200 actions as found in mantra, of which many are also associated with drawings.

7   Balinese believe that every human being is accompanied from the womb to death and beyond by four spirit siblings, male or female depending on gender.

Figure 29 This fine drawing of two intertwined *naga* serpents is called Kaputusan Sanghyang Mretyujana, the 'Perfection of the deity Man of Death'(?). The mantra reads: "ONG Sanghyang Mretyujana blazes out from the fontanel, for I carry off the souls of many 'witches' (*leyak*), not seen by [?]... all are burned up, ya devoured by Sanghyang Mretyujana, ya all bend their knees in defeat, come be silent (*mona*) x3, come let it be so (*poma*) x3." (A *leyak* is believed to be a spirit being created through sorcery or a transformation of the sorcerer). It is to be used in a sash (or amulet); if it is not for siblings, grandchildren or parents (in other words, close family), it should not be given (used), otherwise you would be cursed by it. Bali, probably 1935-1945, ink on paper, 34 x 21,5 cm. NMVW no. RV-4844-116; Hooykaas 1980a illustration no. 301. Photo: Irene de Groot.

Enchanted world: invisible forces and spirits

Daan van Kampenhout

The oldest shaman coats held by museums in Western Europe and Russia date from the seventeenth century. There is no evidence how long these garments, and other paraphernalia like drums, have been used, but many scientists suggest that shamanistic objects were already present in prehistory based on the interpretation of petroglyphs. Of course, this does not mean that there is an uninterrupted tradition. However, information from eighteenth- and nineteenth-century sources suggest that the shamans of Siberia and Mongolia donned special regalia to lead healing ceremonies. When a shaman wore such a magical costume, he transformed from a mere human being into a representation and embodiment of the powers of the universe, of which the material plane is just one dimension. The healing process undertaken by the shaman included a spiritual journey through layered worlds inhabited by all kinds of benevolent and evil spirits. The enhancement of the shaman's costume by amulets, bells and images of protective helping spirits ensured the shaman a relatively safe travel through the other worlds. The costume embodied a universe in a dynamic balance, and through it physical reality could be made orderly and harmonious. The costume was also an armour that protected the shaman against the attacks of evil spirits. In particular the attachments of iron bones fortified the shaman's skeleton, and the use of bronze mirrors warded off evil influences. Through the presence of animals represented in various forms, including birds made of iron and the claws of bears or birds of prey, the shaman could access the powers of these animals. The costume was also a place where spirits live.

The National Museum of World Cultures in Leiden holds an old Siberian shaman coat of the Yakut, in which all aspects mentioned above can be seen. On the back of the coat, the layers of the universe are shown in the form of horizontal leather strips. From it, a multitude of iron hangers dangle, representing the moon and sun, bird feathers and two bears. On the front of the costume there are many objects made from iron: ribs, a collarbone and birds of different shapes. Some of these bird figures represent loons, who can fly through the air, walk on the earth and plunge in deep water. The loon's ability to fly high and dive deep helped the shaman to travel through the upper and lower worlds.

Shaman costumes display considerable regional and individual variation. Among some of the Siberian peoples, the costume consisted of a coat, breast covering, boots, gloves and a headpiece. For other peoples, the costume was only a coat or a belt. Materials could vary as well: the Yakut, for example, had costumes made almost entirely of leather and iron, while others used textiles, beads and parts of animals. Within each cultural group, the shaman's costume fitted that cultural matrix but at the same time there were many individual characteristics.

Figure 30 Shaman's coat, Yakut, Siberia, 1800-1830. Leather, iron, sinew, 134 x 150 cm. NMVW no. RV-1-1582. Photo: Ben Grishaver.

In the exhibition Healing Power, a shaman's coat was on display with headdress, which comes from the Khotgoid, a people living in northwestern Mongolia. This costume is part of my private collection. Several hundred textile 'snakes' are hanging from the back, sides and front. Some of these have special significance, such as the red snake that is considerably thicker than all others dangling at the centre of the backside of the costume. Only the shamans who came from a bloodline of shamans were allowed to suspend this kind of snake on their costumes. In addition, there are also claws of a big owl and a large red dragon made of textile at the back of the coat. Bundles of owl feathers are attached to the shoulders and red triangular pieces of cloth are attached under the arms. These indicate the shaman's skill to fly through the other worlds.

This Mongolian costume has been in my home for about twenty years, together with another old shaman costume, some drums and other original shamanic objects. All of these appeared first in my dreams when I was sleeping, and as I found them in physical reality I recognized them and knew I could welcome them in my house. I see them as guests who have chosen to stay with me rather than as possessions. I clean the costumes regularly with smoke and feed them in ways I have learned from traditional shamans. Shaman costumes have always been regarded as storehouses of spiritual power, as they absorb and collect all the powers at the disposal of the shaman, but they are more than their individual elements: as a whole, the regalia somehow gain a life of their own.

Some years ago, my partner and I were going on vacation and during these weeks a friend lived in our house temporarily. Before I left, I spoke to the costumes and objects, explaining them that I would be gone for a few weeks: 'Please, be kind to the friend who will stay here for a while, as he is invited by us. He comes as a welcome guest; his intentions are good. He will share the house with you for a little while and he is welcome. Please welcome him as well'. And then I proceeded with an improvised prayer: 'All you beautiful old spirits, may you protect the house. May you be undisturbed here in your home, where you have chosen to come and live. May I find you in good condition on my return, when I will stand here again and speak to you to let you know I have returned'.

A week later, when I was basking in the sunshine on a beach far away, my mobile phone rang. Answering the call I heard the distressed voice of my friend, saying: 'Daan, there is a problem here, I need your help...' He explained that he had invited a guest over for dinner. After the meal, this guest had gone to the toilet but quite some time had passed and he hadn't come back to the living room. My friend became

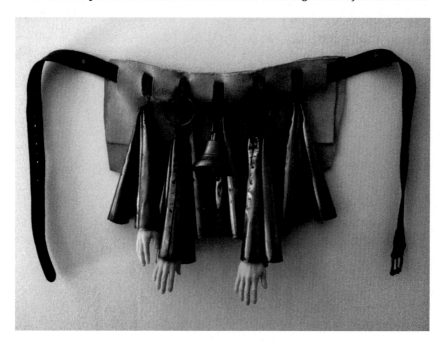

Figure 31 Belt by Daan van Kampenhout. Photo: Daan van Kampenhout.

worried, and finally knocked on the door to inquire if everything was OK. His guest could hardly speak, but managed to say: 'I am scared! I can't move! It is as if several pairs of invisible hands are keeping me in place. It's terrible!' My friend didn't know what to do except to call me. Listening to him, I realized I had made a mistake: I had asked the spirits connected to the old objects to welcome my friend, but had forgotten to mention that any guests he himself might bring in the house would also be welcome. 'Please take your phone to the central altar in my room, and put it there for a moment', I asked my friend. Then I spoke, long distance, to the spirits:

> All you powers that have gathered in my home, I hear how wonderfully you are protecting the place. I am grateful for the work you do and to hear about your strength. But, spirits, I should have told you that the friends of my friend are also welcome in our home. You did a great job, but you can release this man: he is a friend as well.

As I was speaking to the spirits in this way via the phone, my friend heard the toilet door open down the hall, and his guest running for the front door and leaving the house as fast as he could, throwing the front door closed with a loud bang. I added: 'Thank you, spirits, that was a great job – and thanks even more for releasing him!'.

Figure 32 Bird costume by Daan van Kampenhout. Photo: Daan van Kampenhout.

In my work as visual artist, the old shaman costumes have been a source of great inspiration. Their beauty touches me, their spiritual power impresses me, and the vision and skill used in designing and creating them are sometimes nothing less than extraordinary. The costumes can, at best, be only partially understood by people who were not born into the cultures in which they were created. The original costumes will continue to guard their own mysteries. Still, as a Western man, I can do my best to expand my understanding. If we approach the spirits with respect and honesty, the powers of the other worlds might notice our attempts at gaining wisdom, and they may respond through dreams and inspirations that guide us.

One of the ways I study shamanism is by creating ritual costumes and objects myself. But rather than trying to create the kaleidoscopic complexity of a traditional shaman costume, I sometimes focus on just one single spiritual function of the shaman's regalia and build a costume around it. In the Healing Power exhibition, there is an example of such work: a costume that focusses on the shaman's ability to fly, in which boots, coat and headdress make up a bird costume. Hundreds of small plastic birds hang from the back and front of the coat, attached to horizontal layers of textiles representing the layers of the universe. The birds fly through the lower, middle and upper world. The leather is green, referring to the colour of leaves; a plant motif on the fabric, its colour and form represent the great Tree of Life that connects all worlds. Obviously it is not a traditional shaman's costume, and it isn't intended to be so. But through the process of research and slow creation over many days of work, my understanding and appreciation of shamanic traditions keep on growing.

'AYAHUASCA'
VAN HEILIGE PLANT
TOT GLOBALISERING

..ASCA
SACRED PLANT
.OBALISATION

3 Museum magic

Cunera Buijs and Wouter Welling

Today it is generally accepted that objects can be more than their material. Especially ethnographic museums are dealing with this aspect of their collections. In nineteenth- and twentieth-century scientific discourses, the term 'magic' was applied to phenomena connected to the manipulation of supernatural powers. The terms 'black magic' and 'white magic' stem from Euro-American cultures and are foreign to many indigenous ones. The phenomena to which these terms are applied are more complex than a simple dichotomy, as the powers involved can be applied for different purposes and are not, per se, dangerous (bad) or helpful (good).

Objects can be mediators to communicate between realms. However, as indigenous peoples explain, objects can be so much more; they can be alive and inspirited on their own (see Buijs 2018; Clifford 2013; Holsbeke and Rooijakkers 1996; Jakobsen 1999; Welling 2009). For example, in Congo, *minkisi* (singular: *nkisi*) are anthropomorphic sculptures, inhabited by spirits, that are charged with power. *Nkisi* are given life by means of a magical substance, *bilongo*, usually placed in the head, the belly or the back, and often hidden behind a mirror. The mirrors that cover the *bilongo* and the glass eyes make the *nkisi* and its user clairvoyant. With a piece of metal, for example a nail, the *nkisi* can be activated; this can also be done by insulting the sculpture, pouring liquor over it or by exploding gunpowder in its vicinity (Raymakers 2010, 20-23).[1] Ritual specialists, *nganga*, hold this knowledge and activate the *nkisi*.

Within the European context, as well, we find examples of objects being alive. Trees, stones and places in the landscape, such as crossroads, were considered sacred and charged with spiritual powers. The Dutch culture-historian and ethnologist Gerard Rooijakkers (1996, 26) writes:

Figure 33 Bilongo, power object. Container of a strong spiritual force that can be used as protection against diseases or to ward off evil influences. The mirror functions as a window through which the spirit can look outside or the nganga (ritual specialist) can find the cause of the disease. It usually contains natural materials such as white and red earth, bones, resin, seeds. Congo, end 19th century, 10 x 21 x 71 cm. NMVW no. WM-3018. Photo: Irene de Groot.

In the right aisle of Saint Lambert's Church in Meerhoven to the south of Eindhoven [Netherlands], there is a chapel dedicated to Our Lady which is completely dominated by an enormous tree. Where the trunk of the oak branches, a fifteenth-century statue of the Virgin has been placed in a tiny chapel. A large number of silver ex-voto gifts and other kinds of offerings such as rosaries and neck chains with crucifixes have been hung from the lowest branches of the bare tree. This is the cult site of Our Lady of the Oak. According to legend . . . a villager found the statue in an oak tree at this place in 1264. He took it home with him, but three times it returned itself, to its original finding place. The message was clear: it was the Virgin's wish to be worshiped only in that particular place.

Another example of experiencing energy in objects is a 1995 performance of the artist Marina Abramović. She visited the Pitt Rivers Museum in Oxford. At the museum, she received permission to hold her hands above various magical objects in order to feel their power (see Welling, this volume).

Cunera Buijs writes in her contribution 'Powerful Things' (this chapter) about the experience of those who can sense a 'power' connected to sacred and healing-related objects. She describes a researcher experiencing this when studying the nineteenth-century Siberian collection of the National Museum of World Cultures. Similarly, another researcher visiting the permanent exhibition of the National Museum of Ethnology (now part of the National Museum of World Cultures) in Leiden felt energy connected to those museum objects. Although placed in showcases and far from their place of origin, such objects were still 'active'. Buijs explores what material culture can mean to Siberian peoples nowadays and how they interpret their shamanic heritage.

That objects can have 'healing power' comes also to the fore in the articles of Ulrike Bohnet who worked with the Siberian artist Anatoly Donkan. Kept from his ancestral lands and his family while compelled to attend residential school, he lost not only his parents but also his Nanai language and part of his culture. Now making art using old techniques, like tanning fish skin and woodcarving, he shows the strength of material culture and its healing capacities.

In order to reactivate museum objects through ritual activity, Dutch artist Boris van Berkum scans objects from the National Museum of World Cultures' collections. He reworks and samples them on his computer and then fabricates them using a 3D printer. Doing so, he has created a new mask based on a Yoruba mask of the Afrika Museum, explains Markus Balkenhol (this chapter). In 2013, Van Berkum's Kabra mask was then used in rituals in Amsterdam on the 150th anniversary of the abolition of slavery. He convincingly connected the ritual to a collective healing, related both to the enslaved people in the traumatic past of Surinam and the living cultural heritage of Amsterdam. Every year since, the mask is given on loan from the Amsterdam Museum's collection and used in the Keti Koti Festival, commemorating the abolition of slavery.

Claudia Augustat did research among the Piaroa in Venezuela, and found that the production of masks, formerly only used in sacred and shamanic contexts, is now influenced by the demand of the international market and tourists visiting the area. Due to the presence of outsiders and the commercialization of the masks, some Piaroa stopped celebrating their sacred rituals and shamanic practices. Augustat writes, 'Sharing the [sacred] knowledge with strangers was regarded as a loss'.

References

Buijs, Cunera. 2018. "Living objects, The Transfer of Knowledge through East Greenlandic Material Culture." In *Traditions, Traps and Trends, Transfer of Knowledge in Arctic Cultures*, edited by Jarich Oosten and Barbara Helen Miller. Alberta: Polynya Press / University of Alberta Press, 143-189.

Clifford, J. 2013. *Returns: Becoming Indigenous in the Twenty-First Century.* Cambridge, MA: Harvard University Press.

Holsbeke, Mireille (ed.). 1996. *The object as mediator. On the transcendental meaning of art in traditional cultures.* Antwerpen: Ethnografisch Museum.

Jakobsen, Merete Demant. 1999. *Shamanism. Traditional and Contemporary Approaches to the Mastery of Spirits and Healing.* New York / Oxford: Berghahn Books.

Raymakers, Jan. 2010. "Een wereld in verandering." In *Mayombe, rituele beelden uit Congo*, edited by Jo Tollebeek. Tielt: Lanoo, 20-23.

Rooijakkkers, Gerard. 1996. "Cult circuit in the Southern Netherlands. Mediators between heaven and earth." *The object as mediator. On the transcendental Meaning of Art in Traditional Cultures*, edited by Mireille Holsbeke. Antwerpen: Ethnografisch Museum, 19-48.

Welling, Wouter. 2009. "Encounters at the crossroads." In *Roots & More – the journey of the spirits*, Irene Hübner and Wouter Welling. Berg en Dal: Afrika Museum, 65-179.

Notes
1   Translated from Dutch.

Powerful things, transformations of museum objects, cases from the Arctic

Cunera Buijs

The contributions in this volume address the topic of spirituality in a variety of cultures. For many people the world is inhabited by spirits, nowadays often called 'energy'. Within a culture or subculture, numerous spiritual beings can be identified that are addressed with several local terms.

Terto Ngiviu (in this volume) shows how Inugghuit hunters of northeastern Greenland build special connections with spiritual beings in their surroundings, which frequently were profitable and rendered success in hunting. Piers Vitebsky (1995) and Rane Willerslev (2007) both state that alliances between hunters and animals existed in several Siberian cultures as well. Often hunters dreamed about a particular animal, for example, a female elk, and saw the place in the taiga where it would appear during the hunt. There could also be a sexual relationship between the hunter and the animal.

In the Arctic, not only humans and animals were spiritual beings, but also places in the landscape and inanimate objects may have a spirit-owner or be alive. Waldemar Bogoras, a renowned Russian ethnographer who studied several Siberian peoples, summarizes what a Chukchi shaman explained to him:

> All that exists lives. The lamp walks around. The walls of the houses have voices of their own. Even the chamber-vessel has a separate land and house. The skins sleeping in the bags talk at night. The antlers lying on the tombs arise at night and walk in procession around the mounds, while the diseased get up and visit the living. (Bogoras cited in Hutton 2001, 59)

The first time I was confronted with the idea that material culture might have special, spiritual powers was in 1999 when I visited Chuner Michailovitch Taksami in St. Petersburg. Dr. Taksami was a curator and vice director of the State Museum of Ethnology and Anthropology (Kunstkamera), connected to the Russian Academy of Sciences in St. Petersburg.[1] For many years, we had shared an interest in Nivkh material and spiritual culture of the Amur region. When he had earlier visited the Netherlands, in 1993, he and I had studied the entire Siberian collection at the National Museum of Ethnology in Leiden: more than five hundred objects went through our hands. When I travelled to St. Petersburg in 1999, Taksami invited me to his home in St. Petersburg, where he pointed out a marvellous Nivkh drum kept in a container attached to the wall. I was very excited and curious to take a closer look, so I approached the drum and reached to take it from the wall. But Taksami started to shout, 'Don't touch it, don't touch it! You are a woman!' During our earlier study of similar objects, in the context of the museum, there had been not a single sign of reluctance, nor any warning. But now, at his home, it was clearly different. I asked him to explain this confusing situation to me, and he answered: 'The drum still

Figure 34a Shaman's drum, Nivkh, Southeast Siberia, 1850-1898. Animal skin, wood, 74 x 63 cm. NMVW no. RV-1202-239. Photo: Irene de Groot.

Figure 34b A shaman is treating a sick woman sitting on the sleeping platform. From: Leopold von Schrenck: Reisen und Forschungen im Amur-Lande in den Jahren 1854-1856. Band III. Pl-LXI no. 4. St.Petersburg, K.Akademie der Wissenschaften. 1881. Courtesy Royal Library, The Hague, Netherlands.

contains strong powers. I received it as a private gift from a Nivkh shaman. The drum is still warm; it has not been cooled down'.

Taksami continued, saying that it would be dangerous, as the drum was too strong for me. It could harm me, since I was a woman (and maybe not initiated). Then we discussed the difference between museum objects and indigenous objects kept at home. 'Since you are in charge of the museum collection as a curator', he explained, 'it is not a problem for you to touch sacred objects within the museum building'. Curators are allowed to do that, and I have proved to handle them with care and respect. However, when handling sacred objects in an indigenous context, I would have to follow the local proscriptions.

This means that there is a process of transformation that begins when indigenous spiritual objects enter the museum collection – but the power connected to them might still be there. In 2002, a scientist from Hokkaido University who specialized in the Amur cultures visited the stores of the museum in Leiden. He studied the Adolf Vasilyevich Dattan Collection from the Amur region, sometimes photographing an object for research purposes. After he opened one of the drawers in which some grass

Figure 35 Grass doll used to take away sickness, Oroch, Southeast Siberia,1875-1898. 6,3 x 15 x 34 cm. RV-1202-96. Photo: Ben Grishaver.

dolls were kept, he leapt back, uttering: 'This is powerful stuff'. The dolls had been used to cure ill people, especially children; in the process, Nivkh fathers, mothers or shamans tried to transfer the illness from the child to the grass doll. The doll was then put under a tree in the taiga, and thus the family hoped to get rid of the illness (see Buijs 2009). The Japanese scientist explained that the grass dolls in the museum collection still held the supernatural dangers transferred to them, and his reaction left no doubt that he could feel this power.

That special powers may be connected still to material culture (in and outside of the museums), does not mean necessarily that the traditional meanings connected to them are still alive. Seventy years of communism and suppression of shamans and their spiritual culture have brought about huge changes in the spiritual culture of the Amur people of southeast Siberia. The Russian researcher Tatiana Bulgakova (2013, 220) writes that:

Since the 1990s the Nanai experienced rapid socio-religious changes and turned from traditional shamanism/atheism to different forms of religious practice, which had been brought to them from outside.... The young generation's choice is now not classical shamanism, but rather other religious practices like various forms of New-Age spiritualities, and evangelical Christian movements.

Bulgakova explains that, in many respects, the young Nanai are successors to the shamans, and that among them exists a strong biological-spiritual inheritance. This means that new religions are interpreted as 'various modifications of the shamanic-like experience . . . and [they] explain their native shamanism in terms of the attractive ideas borrowed from other religions' (Bulgakova 2013, 220.) While they rarely use a drum, they are convinced that they work with the same energy processes, interpreted by their forefathers as 'spirits'. Bulgakova (213, 220) notes that the word 'energy' has replaced the old words 'seven' and 'amban' [helping spirits]'. The younger generation of 'new shamans' is using New Age or neo-shamanism vocabulary, but, according to Bulgakova, their night dreams and visions are very similar to those of traditional shamans. One of the neo-shamans Bulgakova spoke with, Marina, explains: 'Cosmos is energy or, in other words, the spirit of the (departed shamans), who had stored a huge base of knowledge and who are now returning that knowledge to us' (Bulgakova 2013, 221).

What does such a process of cultural change, which also occurs globally, mean for the traditional material culture of the Amur region? Many aspects have changed or disappeared from daily life. Traditional dress is now only worn for festive occasions, and shamanic objects have gone out of use. Ulrike Bohnet (in this volume) describes the work and life of the Nanai artist Anatoly Donkan, and how his cultural background is not only a marker for his (lost) indigenous identity and his art but

Figure 36 Anatol Donkan wearing the shaman's coat he made. The costume is now in the collection of the National Museum of World Cultures, Leiden, 2017. Salmon and catfish leather, iron and copper, ink, 148 x 158 cm. NMVW no. 7143-1 t/m 4. Photo: Christine Fottner.

Figure 37 Shaman's coat by Anatol Donkan, 2017, on display in the healing exhibition in 2019, Leiden. Salmon and catfish leather, iron and copper, ink, 148 x 158 cm. NMVW no. 7143-1 t/m 4. Photo: Ben Bekooy.

also a life force. Donkan, who divides his time between St. Petersburg and Viechtach, Germany, designed a shaman's costume and a drum for the National Museum of World Cultures. The costume was made out of fish skin, an old technique from the Amur region, and he used Russian inks and colours from the Factory for Leather in St. Petersburg. The coat, apron and hat were handcrafted with catfish and salmon leather; the crow was framed in iron. The pendants were made of iron, copper, tin and brass. 'All metals have a personal meaning for the shaman', explains Donkan, 'and for every use he has for them. This is my personal combination'. The coat is heavily decorated with pictorial designs, which go back to the spiritual culture of the Nanai, yet it is simultaneously a recent and personal interpretation of the artist. The coat is, according to Donkan, a place for the spirits. In an interview with Ulrike Bohnet, conducted for the National Museum of World Cultures, Donkan explains:

> Every tree, mountain, lake – everything we see – is alive, animated by a spirit. . .
> . There is the world we are living in, Dorkin, and there is Buni, the world of the
> deceased – the underworld. The soul separates herself from the body and moves
> into a little idol, that is made as a house for the soul. . . . In a ceremony, the shaman
> helps to bring the soul of the deceased into the world of the ancestors. This is
> the third existing world, Endur. On the coat you see a toad and a salamander.
> These both can be on the land (earth) and dive under the water [animals that
> can transgress several realms often help the spirits of shamans during travel].

There are mosquitoes depicted on the coat, capable of transporting a soul in a bubble of blood. Snakes can be seen: these own wisdom and can give it to the shaman. The coat is also like a map, depicting places where the shaman can go. It is important that he can find the way and come back to this world. This piece of art is of an astonishing quality and has rich spiritual content.

Bulgakova (2013, 222) writes in her epilogue:

> Reviving shamanism became a brand of identity and is now proclaimed as a
> means of preserving traditional culture. But . . . the representatives of the
> *Association of Indigenous Peoples of the North, Siberia and Far East of the*
> *Russian Federation* are not confused by the fact that the practice of new Nanai
> shamans does not suppose to revive the old shamanic rituals as such, and that
> today the Nanai neo-shaman resembles more a healer, sorcerer and a person of
> extrasensory perception.

In a sense this also holds true for the shamanic-related and identity-reinforcing art of Donkan. It is not by accident that he refers to his art as healing.

References

Buijs, Cunera. 2009. "Powerful stuff, Transformations in Arctic Artifacts." In: *Tra-ditions on the Move. Essays in honour of Jarich Oosten* edited by Sabine Luning, Jan Jansen & Erik de Maaker (eds), 27-46. Amsterdam: Rozenberg Publishers.

Bulgakova, Tatiana. 2013. *Nanai Shamanic Culture in Indigenous Discourse*. Fürsten-berg/Havel: Verlag der Kulturstiftung Siberien/SEC Publications.

Hutton, Ronald. 2001. *Shamans, Siberian Spirituality and the Western Imagination*. London: Hambleton Continuum.

Vitesbsky, Piers. 1995. *The Shaman: voyages of the soul trance, ecstasy and healing from Siberia to the Amazon*. London: D. Baird.

Willerslev, Rane. 2007. *Soul Hunters: Hunting, Animism, and Personhood among the Siberian Yukaghirs*. Berkeley, CA: University of California Press.

Notes

1   Some of the examples mentioned in this article have been published in Buijs 2009.

Roots and the art of healing

Anatoly Donkan and Ulrike Bohnet

'To research and to deal with my Nanai descent goes through whole my life and my artistic work.' (Anatoly Donkan)

The life and work of Anatoly Donkan truly bridges worlds. Born in 1955 in Tunguska, Siberia, Soviet Union, he now lives and works in St. Petersburg, Russia, and Viechtach, Germany, making art, tanning fish skins, carving wood, blacksmithing and painting.

It is all part of his path back to his indigenous roots, with art as key and tool.

His quest started years after growing up in several Soviet state orphanages, not knowing about his Nanai family from whom he was taken. Severed from his roots and native language, educated in Russian and growing up with a Soviet worldview, Donkan graduated from the Marine Akademy of Nachotka, and subsequently worked eight years as helmsman on a fishing fleet cruising the Sea of Okhotsk.

With the decreasing fish stocks and the changes accompanying perestroika, Donkan got the chance for a second education. Following his heart's calling, he studied art in Khabarowsk, graduating in 1992 with a degree in Graphic Art and Education. In this time of often-chaotic adjustments, spaces of liberation emerged as well as possibilities for open-ended and personal discovery. Thus, Donkan found inspiration and space to look into the history and material culture of the Nanai people, supported and empowered by Nanai Historian Nikolai Batunowich Kile. His personal and artistic quest led Donkan to Nanai wooden sculptures, which are outstanding and unique in their composition and manufacture. Deeply fascinated, Donkan plunged into this universe of ancestral figurines, shamanic helping spirits, hunting assistants and family idols, all of which he observed in local ethnographic

Figure 38 Portrait of Anatoly Donkan. Photo: Christine Fottner.

museum collections. Concentrating on the complex shamanic worldview manifested in idols assembled in the museums' basement, he sensed them as orphaned, abstracted from the nourishment of cultural practices, such as commonly shared rituals of feeding and offering. So, for his graduation exhibition, Donkan displayed them, a huge gathering of idols tattooed with collection numbers and silenced by time and neglect. What would have become a scandal in earlier times marked the

Figure 39 House-spirit 'grandmother' by Anatoly Donkan, , Germany, 2018. Wood, glass, textile, 44 × 28 × 28 cm. NMVW no. 7143-6. Photo: Irene de Groot.

start of Donkan's research and quest into the artistic expression of his indigenous roots and Nanai culture.

As a skilled craftsperson, he travelled with artist Mareile Onodera throughout the Lower Amur region to collect impressions, inspirations and oral traditions of the Nanai people in villages and settlements. During these journeys, he became for the first time excited about fish leather, an almost indestructible traditional material, which was once essential in fishing cultures from the Amur region to Sakhalin but has now been mostly replaced by plastic or textiles. In the past called Fishfur-Barbarians by Russian and Chinese traders, Nanai people were famous for their unique art of tanning fish skin into smooth leather and sewing it into elegant robes that were sometimes painted with elaborate ornamentation.[1] In the nineteenth century, fish leather was even produced for museum collections in Europe and America. However, knowledge of the fish leather manufacturing process had almost disappeared by the 1990s. Donkan had to combine the fragmentary instructions he received from Nanai grandmothers with years of trial and error to finally arrive at the method of making the leather. He and Mareile Onodera first worked in the remote Nanai settlement of Kondon for two years. After, he established his studio and workshop in the urban environment of Vladivostok. 'These years taught me a lot about the fantastic skills

Figure 40 Anatoly Donkan is drawing mythical designs on the shaman's coat which he made for the National Museum of World Cultures in Leiden, Netherlands. Photo: Christine Fottner.

Figure 41 Shaman's belt, Oroch, Southeast Siberia, from the Adolph Dattan collection of the National Museum of World Cultures, Leiden. 1850-1898. Leather, iron, 28,8 x 98,5 cm. NMVW no. RV-1202-235. Photo: Irene de Groot.

of my ancestors', Donkan remembers, 'I had to find out how to adapt it to my way of living – how to get the raw skins and how to tan, to soften and to use them'.

Pursuing his practical research about fish leather, he was invited to Austria in 1999 to contribute his knowledge and practical skills to an exhibition of Nanai fish leather objects that belonged to the Vienna Völkerkundemuseum (now Weltmuseum) as part of the Adolph Traugott Dattan (1854-1924) collection. Inspired by these ethnographic objects, which were collected in the beginning of the twentieth century in the Lower Amur region, Donkan created his own fish leather art objects and robes, uniting traditional Nanai compositions with haute couture. Since 2005 he has been well-received with his own style and secrets about how to transform (often wasted) fish skins into high-quality leather. These techniques are increasingly being rediscovered by the fashion industry.

For Donkan the meaning goes far beyond the beauty or sustainability of the material: it is a direct link between him and his Nanai roots, summated by a deep admiration for his ancestors' skills and way of life. For him it also includes a shamanic worldview with its knowledge about balancing, transforming and healing. In his art, Donkan expresses the idea of interwoven worlds and multidimensional realities, animated with his very own interpretations, reflecting and transforming the cultural background he encounters in Nanai objects, stories and materials. Art became his individual tool to get in touch with his ancestral history and his personal link to his roots. It is also a tool for healing, he explains: 'Most of the fellows that grew up with me in those orphanages have died already. Like me, they were removed from their indigenous families, from their traditions, from their cultural identities. They didn't survive being cut off from their roots'.

Donkan's adaption of a shaman's coat made of salmon leather for the exhibition Healing Power is his very own way of creating and opening a whole universe of expressions: a collection of old and new stories, cultural echoes and personal experiences, a map of spirits and landscapes in an inspired multilayered world, a living story about the past and the future.

Notes

1   Глебова Елена: Метаморфозы рыбьей кожи: Путь древнего ремесла народов Амура /Е.В.Глебова; худож. Доротее Логен. - Хабаровск: Омега-Пресс, 2010.

Kabra healing: ancestors and colonial memory in the Netherlands

Markus Balkenhol

When the history of slavery became part of a broader public memory in the Netherlands in the early 1990s, one central concern was the question of healing. Slavery, the descendants of the enslaved argued, had inflicted physical and mental wounds that had not healed. The question of how exactly to treat historical trauma and pain, however, remains unsolved.

It is not surprising that the *kabra*, African-Surinamese ancestors, would involve themselves at this point. People of African-Surinamese descent in the Netherlands regularly turn to their ancestors for all kinds of illnesses, both physical and mental. *Obiaman* or *doeman* (healers) have a flourishing trade in treating problems concerning love, sex, work, mental health and everything else life throws at people. Healers can harness the power of the Winti spirits and the ancestors to help solve these problems. Healing, in other words, is also spirit business.

So in 1998, perhaps not coincidentally the year that the petition for a national slavery memorial was submitted to the Dutch Parliament, the ancestors contacted Marian Markelo, a prominent priestess of the African-Surinamese Winti religion in the Netherlands (see chapter 1 in this volume). They gave her the task to 'bring back' something that was lost during slavery: the religious artefacts of the African ancestors. It was now time, the ancestors said, to restore this tradition, as a way of healing the wounds of the past.

But it was not easy to know what cure exactly the ancestors had in mind, and it took thirteen years to find it. In 2011, Markelo met Boris van Berkum, a Dutch artist based in Rotterdam. Van Berkum had just finished a solo exhibition at the prestigious Museum Boijmans Van Beuningen in Rotterdam. He described their first meeting during a worship as a 'magical moment', in which Markelo, guided by the ancestors, chose Van Berkum as a partner in the project they came to call an 'African Renaissance' in the Winti religion (Balkenhol 2015).

Van Berkum set to work and made a series of what he calls 'African-inspired' sculptures. He realized, however, that these sculptures did not provide the immediate connection with the ancestors he was looking for. People needed to be able to, as it were, dance with and touch the ancestors *through* these works of art. He saw that he, as he told me, had to 'go where the African ancestors live in the Netherlands – in the great African collections of Dutch museums'. Markelo and Van Berkum went to the Afrika Museum in Berg en Dal, where the ancestors guided them to a number of masks in the depot, which they then 'liberated'. First, two masks were scanned with a portable Artec 3D scanner, a device that dissolves a material object into 'point cloud coordinates,' a mass of raw data that digitally defines the shape of the object. Then, the raw data was computer-rendered. Finally,

Figure 42 Yoruba Egungun mask representing an ancestor. West-Africa, date unknown. Wood, iron, 9 cm x 17,5 cm x diam. 20,5 cm. NMVW no. AM-481-5. Photo: Ferry Herrebrugh.

Figure 43 Kabra ancestor mask by Boris van Berkum, 2013. Lacquered polyurethane, batik textile, wood, 66 x 40 x 40 cm. Amsterdam Museum Collection. Amsterdam. Photo: Erik Hesmerg.

the masks were milled in polyurethane foam. One of them was transformed into a 1.5-meter-high dancing mask ('Papa Winti'). The other, which I discuss in this chapter, was incorporated into a six-meter-high sculpture of Mama Aisa ('Mama Aisa XXXL') and also transformed into a 66 x 40 x 40 cm *kabra* mask. This wooden, anthropomorphic mask with large, half-moon shaped eyes and an iron earring (9 x 17.5 x 20.5 cm) originated in the Yoruba region in Nigeria. It was used in the *Egungun* (lit. 'mask') cult, a secret society of masqueraders. The society used these masks in ancestor worship (Beier 1958), but they were also part of secular theatrical performances at the Royal Court (Adedeji 1972).

Only the shape remained of the original piece, and the new *kabra* mask needed to be a sensation. It was decided that it should be considerably larger: 'The original model was too small, it would not have produced the kind of presence [*aanwezigheid*] we were looking for,' Van Berkum explained to me. 'In an African village, you have maybe thirty people, but we were looking for a public of three hundred or more. And it also has to do well on television'.

Figure 44 Kabra ancestor dance mask performs during the libation by Marian Markelo in the Oosterpark in Amsterdam, 2013, at the National Commemoration of the 150th anniversary of the abolition of slavery. Photo: James van den Ende.

Moreover, Van Berkum also radically changed the appearance of the mask: instead of the original wooden colour he applied transparent polyurethane varnish, through which the light-beige hue of the polyurethane foam is visible.[1] On top of the varnish, Van Berkum blew brass powder, then sanded it so that only golden-tinted dots are visible on the mask's surface. The piece is dressed in blue-and-white *persie* (a type of cloth whose white and blue colours and patterns refer to the ancestors), which is glued on top of its head, thus reminiscent of a head-tie. Around the neck, the mask wears a collar of tulle, hiding a wooden structure so it can be worn on top of the head. The mask was unveiled in 2013, and has since appeared during ancestor worship ceremonies and the annual celebration of abolition in Amsterdam (Balkenhol 2015, 252 ff.).

So what kind of healing are these masks doing? With their message to Markelo, the ancestors had gone far beyond the treatment of physical bodies to concern themselves with social bodies: the Winti community, the descendants of the enslaved in the Netherlands, and ultimately the Dutch nation. Social healing of historical trauma and pain includes but is not limited to the biomedical focus on the individual and thus requires holistic techniques that address the person as embedded in and emerging from social relations. The idea that a person's well-being is deeply connected to the social and spiritual worlds is at the heart of the Winti tradition (Wekker 2006; Wooding 1972). In making the *kabra* mask, Markelo and Van Berkum

Figure 45 Mama Aisa by Boris van Berkum, 2020. Marian Markelo posed for this sculpture. Polyesther with goldleaf 150 x 100 x 125 cm. Computer render.

have chosen the intersecting processes of heritagization and sacralization (Meyer and de Witte 2013).

Writing about cultural heritage and the sacred, Birgit Meyer and Marleen de Witte have introduced the twin notions of the 'heritagization of the sacred' and the 'sacralization of heritage'. 'Heritagization of the sacred' looks at 'how religious traditions become represented and recognized (or contested and rejected) in the framework of "heritage"' (Meyer and de Witte 2013, 277). Heritagization is a complex process in the case of the *kabra* mask. The wooden masks of the Afrika Museum had already undergone a process of heritagization when they were taken out of their West African context by missionaries and placed into a museum in the nineteenth century. Markelo and Van Berkum redefined these museum objects as objects of 'African heritage' that had been lost during slavery and that were to play a crucial role in the healing process. Then the *kabra* mask attained yet another layer of heritage, when it was acquired by the Amsterdam Museum in 2013. As the museum curator, Annemarie de Wildt, argued, the mask not only referred to the history of the city but was itself turned into an object of cultural heritage because of its presence at the city's historic 150th anniversary of the abolition of slavery. 'Healing', in this case, refers to repairing a representational gap. The mask symbolically stands for a group of Amsterdam's citizens who feel misrepresented in the museum. Now a part of the museum's collection, the mask is meant to fill that gap, thus changing the heritage canon of the city itself.

The masks were not only meant to safeguard cultural heritage but also to constitute a process of sacralization. In 'bringing back' the sacred objects of the African ancestors, Markelo and Van Berkum aimed to restore sacredness to the Winti religion. Winti had been rejected especially by Protestants in Suriname as superstition and idol worship, a position that many people of African-Surinamese descent have internalized. Winti, Markelo argues, had lost its sacredness, and the masks were a way of conveying to people that Winti is not black magic or witchcraft, but a comprehensive cosmology and engagement with the divine. 'Sacralization', Meyer and de Witte (2013, 277) explain, refers to 'how certain heritage forms become imbued with a sacrality that makes them appear powerful, authentic, or even incontestable'. The masks are specifically designed to evoke an immediate connection with the ancestors and to instil a religious sensation in the practitioners.

It remains to be seen whether the masks as techniques of postcolonial healing will indeed be able to cure the wounds of the past, but they already show that healing the colonial past demands collectively imagining different futures. The masks also show that the ancestors, in the past, present and future, can be important agents in such a process.

References

Balkenhol, Markus. 2015. "Working with the Ancestors. The Kabra Mask and the 'African Renaissance' in the Afro-Surinamese Winti Religion." *Material Religion: The Journal of Objects, Art and Belief* 11 (2), 250-54.

Meyer, Birgit, and Marleen de Witte. 2013. "Heritage and the Sacred: Introduction." *Material Religion: The Journal of Objects, Art and Belief* 9 (3), 274-80.

Wekker, Gloria. 2006. *The Politics of Passion: Women's Sexual Culture in the Afro-Surinamese Diaspora*. Columbia University Press.

Wooding, C. J. 1972. *Winti, Een Afro-Amerikaanse Godsdienst in Suriname*. Meppel: Krips Repro.

Notes

1   Some of the examples mentioned in this article have been published in Balkenhol 2015.

Shamanism in transition: ritual masks among the Piaroa

Claudia Augustat

In 1995, a Piaroa man, living in a small community on the Sipapo River in the Venezuelan Amazon, died of an unidentified disease. The Piaroa understand disease as the result of inappropriate behaviour toward spiritual beings or attacks from shamans. The latter is what Neal L. Whitehead and Robin Wright (2004: 3) call 'the dark side of shamanism', meaning that killing and curing are complementary rather than opposed. In this case, the people in the region believed that the man was killed through the interventions of shamans, because he presented and sold masks used in the *warime* ritual to tourists. The *warime* was the central ritual of the Piaroa and a binding element of a social group sharing a territory.[1] It connected the present to the mythical time of creation, and the secular to the sacred, and it provided the vernacular with virtue. The masks were ritual instruments.

Figure 46 Headdress, Piaroa, Venezuela, South-America. Before 1968, feathers, plant materials, 70 × 25 × 29cm. NMVW no. TM-3764-6. Photo: Irene de Groot.

Their origin is traced back to mythical times and to the cultural hero *Wahari*. In the *warime* ritual, they manifested the possibility to cross the border between the present and mythical time. In the terms of Maurice Godelier (1999: 200) they are sacred objects excluded from exchange. According to the Piaroa, the masks are sacred because of their mythical origin and their creation under ritual circumstances. They are the group's inalienable property.

There were two kind of shamans among the Piaroa: the *meneruwa*, who is mainly a healer, and the *yuweweruwa* or the religious specialist. The shaman who was responsible for the *warime* and the creation of the ritual masks was the *yuweweruwa*. But, like the *meneruwa* he possessed the ability to heal through the power of songs, the *mene*. The *yuweweruwa* played an essential role in the reproduction of society and culture among the Piaroa, combining political and spiritual leadership.

The *meneruwa* had the responsibility of purifying the prey from spiritual pathogens with the *mene*. Anxiety about disease and protecting against it was part of daily life among the Piaroa. If this was already true in pre-contact times (before the eighteenth century), it is easy to imagine how it increased after the Piaroa's

Figure 47 Model of a mask dancer. Piaroa, Venezuela, South-America. Made before 1999. Photo: Claudia Augustat.

encounter with missionaries and representatives from the national government. After the 1940s, epidemics created crises for the Piaroa. At the beginning of the 1970s many Piaroa sought a better and safer life, leaving their homes in the forest and moving closer to criollo villages, missions and Puerto Ayacucho, the capital of the then territory of Amazonas. Simultaneously, the government started a development programme and promised to support indigenous peoples if they left their homes. Unfortunately, most of these promises were not kept. The Piaroa tried to make the best of the new situation with the support of the Salesian Fathers and the New Tribes Mission. They started producing crops for the market, sent their children to school and in the 1980s developed political organizations to obtain a better position in the 'struggle' with the national government. As part of this development, the shamans continued to lose power while new elites, who were trained in the mission schools and spoke fluent Spanish, emerged (Oldham 1996).

These developments led to a devaluation of the knowledge of the sacred masks among the younger generation. Out of fear it was no longer possible to celebrate the *warime* ritual properly and benefit the whole community, some Piaroa decided to give up the ritual altogether or to increase secrecy towards other Piaroa. These decisions contributed to the fading of the ritual, but there is no proof that it ever disappeared completely.

Figure 48 Atelier of artist Alfonso Peres in Paria Grande, Venezuela. 1999. Photo: Claudia Augustat.

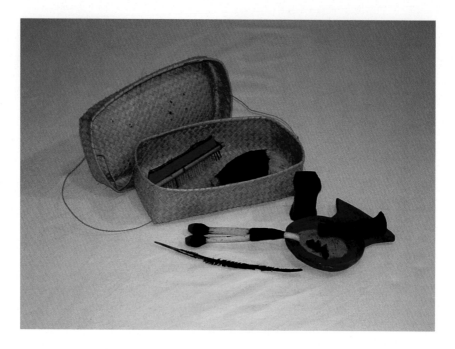

Figure 49 Set for snuffing *yopo*. Collection Augustat, Piaroa, Venezuela, South-America, 2000. Photo: Claudia Augustat.

Considering that a discourse about making and selling masks to tourist developed in the 1990s, it would appear that the *warime* ritual is still alive at least as a concept in some communities. The discourse is embedded in the traditional values of the Piaroa. In Paria Grande, the centre of the mask production, the artists made them with the permission of the shaman.

To legitimize the sale of masks, iconographic details were altered. Masks produced for sale were made at home by an individual artist who was also their owner. Natural material was transformed into an image of a spiritual being, as in traditional masks, but without the influence of *yopo* (*Anadenanthera peregrina),* a psychoactive substance. Without *yopo,* the door to mythical time was closed and the image remained powerless.

Most artists had never tried *yopo* and lacked any experience of the mythical and spiritual world as a reality. Their understanding of relationships with mythical beings was thus a memory of an ancient lifestyle. Still, this memory was part of their identity, and they used the masks to keep a distinctive material culture alive in the multiethnic art market of Puerto Ayacucho.

For those opposed to making masks for sale, in particular those in the region around Autana Tepui, these arguments were not valid. For them, the ritual masks

Figure 50 The ghost of the peccari and the monkey are part of the original masks created by Wahari. Mask of the monkey spirit. Piaroa, Venezuela, South-America. Before 1968, plant materials, 80 × 30 × 20cm. NMVW no. TM-3764-18. Photo: Irene de Groot.

were not merely images, but were continuous with the original masks created by *Wahari* in mythic time.

Moreover, by selling the masks, a piece of the secret cultural knowledge of the Piaroa was sold. They also regarded the sharing of knowledge with strangers, with anthropologists and especially with tourists, as a loss. Perhaps some Piaroa would agree with Annette Weiner (1985, 211) when she writes:

> Keeping things instead of giving them away is essential if one is to retain some measure of one's social identity in the face of potential loss. . . . But a loss may indicate a perceived weakness in a group's identity and therefore in its power to sustain itself for future generations. Such a loss is a destruction of the past, which ultimately weakens the future.

The divergent arguments for selling the masks or guarding knowledge about them reflect the different strategies to preserve culture and formulate a distinctive identity as used in Paria Grande and the region around Autana Tepui. These strategies included participating in political organizations, sharing the culture with strangers, as well as maintaining strict boundaries and secrecy. The mask as a symbol of identity was a powerful instrument used by both parties: on one side, to gain acceptance through adjustment, on the other, to keep control over cultural knowledge and to assert autonomy by preserving distance.

The conflict over the commodification of masks only superficially touches on the selling of sacred objects. The central question is: what role should the mask play in the preservation of Piaroa culture? Depending on the social interactions in which they are used, legitimation is sought by permitting or banning the sale of the *warime* masks.

In 2009, I returned to Puerto Ayacucho. At the airport, human-size sculptures of the *warime* masks welcomed visitors. This was a surprise because ten years earlier, during my fieldwork, the mask business had been kept rather secretive out of fear of shamanic attacks. I heard that the shaman of Paria Grande had died a few years earlier, leaving the business unregulated, and there had been few shamanic apprentices to take his place. During my short stay, it was not possible to research whether shamans were still active among the Piaroa and what happened to the *warime* ritual. The living conditions of indigenous peoples are changing today, sometimes rapidly. Therefore and because the article is based on fieldwork for my PhD thesis, which was conducted between 1999 and 2000, I have written this article in the past tense to emphasize the connections between ritual and history.

References

Augustat, Claudia. 2006. *Entmachtete Gegenstände? Zur Kommerzialisierung sakraler Masken bei den Piaroa in Venezuela*. Veröffentlichungen zum Archiv für Völkerkunde 12. Wien: LIT-Verlag.

Boglár, L. 1985. *Wahari. Eine südamerikanische Urwaldkultur*. Hanau: Müller und Kiepenheuer.

Godelier, M. 1999. *The Enigma of the Gift*. Chicago: University of Chicago Press and Polity Press.

Kaplan Overing, J. 1975. *The Piaroa. A People of the Orinoco Basin. A Study in Kinship and Marriage*. Oxford: Clarendon Press.

Oldham, P. 1996. *The Impacts of Development and Indigenous Response among the Piaroa of the Venezuelan Amazon*. University of London: Unpublished Thesis.

Weiner, Annette. 1985. "Inalienable wealth." *American Ethnologist* 12(2), 210-227.

Whitehead, N. L. and Wright R. 2004. "Introduction: Dark Shamanism." In: *In Darkness and Secrecy. The Anthropology of Assault Sorcery and Witchcraft in Amazonia*. N. L. Whitehead and R. Wright (Eds.). Durham and London: Duke University Press, 1-19.

Notes

1   My description of the culture and rituals of the Piaroa is based on the work of Boglár (1985) and Kaplan Overing (1975).

4 Balance and harmony

Cunera Buijs and Wouter Welling

In many shamanic traditions, balance and (dis)harmony are not only related to individual behaviour but also to that of society, because individual attitudes affect the group. Transgressions of rules and taboos can distort relationships with the spiritual world and the ancestors. This may lead to illness, hunger, bad weather and other complications (Oosten 1997; Anderson 2011; De Smet 1999; Vitebsky 2001). According

Figure 51 Young Mentawaian shaman with ornaments, Indonesia, 1895 Photo: C.B. Nieuwenhuis, 1895. NMVW no. TM-10005477.

to Reimar Schefold (this chapter), a Dutch anthropologist who did a lifetime of research among the Mentawai in Indonesia, 'every person has to take care of his soul. The soul expects from the human being: a beautiful [harmonious] lifestyle in daily life with ornaments, tranquillity and good food, and, during the ritual periods, festive dances and artistic performances'.

Among the Ayuuk people in Mexico, Juan Carlos Reyes Gómez explains (in this chapter), there are different concepts of being well or being happy. During religious celebrations, the Ayuuk people ask to be free from problems or misfortune by begging the Gods to allow them to be *jantsytsuj-hantsyyajkxon*, which means 'being well in a beautiful way'. Balance and harmony are key concepts in the well-being of the entire community. A holistic worldview prevails in which nature, the gods, the divine and human beings are interconnected, and the community holds sway over the individual.

In the Netherlands there is a growing search for 'alternative' healing practices. People today experience the constraints of an achievement-oriented society, causing

Figure 52 Skirt of a shaman, Sakudei, Indonesia, ca. 1950. Cotton, mother-of-pearl, rotan, feathers, 58 × 58cm, NMVW no. 7086-128. Photo: Irene de Groot.

burnouts and stress-related illnesses. People consult not only the medical doctors but also get inspired and helped by healing traditions from other parts of the world. Maria Van Daalen was initiated in Haiti as a Manbo Asogwe (a Haitian Vodou priestess in the highest degree of initiation). She assists clients with stress, pain, depression, etc., and explains (this chapter): 'An important word in the practice of Haitian Vodou is *"balanse"* [bah-lahn-SAY]. We bring back the balance in the life of the client, we balance her/him'.

References

Anderson, David G. 2011. "Introduction, Local Healing Landscapes." In *The Healing Landscapes of Central and Southern Siberia*, edited by David G. Anderson. Alberta: The University of Alberta Press, 1-13.

De Smet, Peter, 1999. *Herbs, Health, Healers. Africa as ethnopharmacological treasury*. Berg en Dal: Afrika Museum.

Oosten, Jarich. 1997. "Amulets, shamanic clothes and paraphernalia in Inuit culture." In *Braving the cold, Continuity and change in Arctic clothing*, edited by Cunera Buijs & Jarich Oosten. Leiden: Research School CNWS, 105-131.

Vitebsky, Piers. 2001. *Shamanism*. Norman: University of Oklahoma Press.

Aakujk'äjt-Jotkujk'äjtën: balance and harmony in *Ayuuk* culture

Juan Carlos Reyes Gómez

Introduction, the Ayuuk people

This paper is about the concept *aakujk'äjt-jotkujk'äjtën*, which in Ayuuk culture refers to the idea of 'being well'.[1] In Ayuuk language, these concepts form a *difrasismo* or two words mostly used together, in the same sequence, applied in similar contexts and functioning as one single expression, meaning they constitute one unit of significance.[2]

As we shall see, this culture holds a holistic or comprehensive view on matters. Everything is interrelated, nothing is isolated; all parts must work well to have the whole functioning correctly. One wrong part in the whole will affect all parts.

This view includes the physical-mental-spiritual areas of being, but goes far beyond the person to encompass the family and community. As we can see, the community aspect prevails over the individual one; the goal is to prioritize the interests of the community over personal or family benefit. Of course, this does not mean that communities are free from problems. Distinct personal, family,

Figure 53 Depositing offerings to the Ayuuk gods before an altar, at the priest's house, asking for care and protection. Photo: L. Reyes, 2012.

intracommunity and intercommunity problems must be confronted. However, they are but the product of negligence in the Balance and the Harmony that need to be taken care of and maintained.

Moreover, to be well in Ayuuk culture is more than simply not suffering from physical or mental ailments. The relation between health and illness is considered within the balance or equilibrium that all must reach so as to attain Harmony with the whole, that is with our gods and other divine beings, with nature, with our fellow beings and with ourselves. Doing so will allow us to reach maturity, plenitude, wisdom – that is to be *really* well, to live well beyond all things material. This wellness is, at heart, a spiritual matter.

About the Ayuuk people

The Ayuuk people, just like the Zoque and Popoluca people, are of ancient Olmec descent, the culture that developed the greatest and oldest Mesoamerican civilization (Campbell and Kaufman 1976; Justeson and Kaufman 1993; Kaufman and Justeson 2001). Recent linguistic and archaeological studies have demonstrated that the Olmecs, and their ancestors (the Mokaya or the Corn People), spoke an old version of the language still used today by the Ayuuk, Zoque and Popoluca (Pérez 2012; Pohl et al. 2002; Clark and Blake 1989; Pye and Clark 2006).

Before the sixteenth century, when the European invasion occurred, the Ayuuk had continuously fought against the neighbouring Zapotecs, Mixtecs and Mexicas, other indigenous people of Mexico, to defend their freedom. After the European invasion, the Ayuuk people endured persecution and relentless harassment of the Spanish soldiers and missionaries who wanted to snatch their territory, loot their natural resources, and enslave them, as well as force them to give up their own religion and adopt Christianity as the only form of spiritual expression. But the Ayuuk had long known how to defend their territory and liberty, having fought against their neighbours to preserve not only their natural resources but also their own language, culture, world vision, religion, philosophy and wisdom.

Presently, five centuries after this invasion, the Ayuuk continue to preserve a considerable amount of their linguistic and cultural patterns, but they continue to suffer exterior threats of extermination, in a globalizing world with transnational companies and a capitalistic system, tending towards cultural and linguistic homogenization, industrialization and accumulation of capital, even at the cost of exploitation and death of entire peoples and the destruction of the world itself.

Consequently, the Ayuuk keep on struggling to preserve their language and culture, as well as their specific forms of social and political organization. At the same time they demand respect for and observance of the rights of indigenous peoples, including the right not to be discriminated against, assimilated, forcibly displaced and exterminated; the right to have an honourable and fair life; the right to be consulted

Figure 54 Blouse, made by the Kojpëtë, a weaving and dyeing school in the Mixe (Ayuuk) town of Tlahuitoltepec, Oaxaca, Mexico. Cotton, machine embroidered. 2016, 70 × 148cm. NMVW no. 7098-1. Photo: Irene de Groot.

about any project the state wishes to implement on their land and territories, and to refuse such plans if necessary; and above all, the right of sovereignty.

The expression 'aakujk'äjt-jotkujk'äjtën'

The expression 'aakujk'äjt-jotkujk'äjtën' does not necessarily imply 'to be happy', 'contented' or 'joyful' but conveys the idea of being 'without sorrow', 'without anxiety', 'without problems', 'without any worries'. It is being serene, peaceful, calm. In general terms, it refers to 'the fact of being in balance and harmony' with all that surrounds us.

'Ijtën-xo'onën' or simply 'xontääkën' expresses joy or happiness and 'mo'onën-tujkën' refers to sadness and worry; to allude to anxiety and desperation, 'mä'äyën-täjën' is used. To denote problems and misfortune, the *difrasismo* 'ayo'on-jotmay' is used, while 'yuu-pä'äm' is utilized to refer to illnesses.

During the celebration of religious events, people ask to be free of problems or misfortune, using the *difrasismo* 'nitii'ayo'on-nitiijotmayë', begging the gods to allow the Ayuuk to be *jantsytsuj-jantsyyajkxon* (very well, in a beautiful way) and *jantsy'aakujk-jantsyjotkujk* (without problems or worries; *really well*).[3]

Figure 55 Blouse designed by Isabel Marant, based on the original Mixe blouse. Spring/summer collection 2015. The designer was accused of cultural appropriation. Cotton, wool, machine embroidered. 2015. 97 × 155cm. NMVW no. 7043-1. Photo: Irene de Groot.

Being really well

'To be *really well*' is to be in balance in the physical, mental and spiritual fields on a personal, family and community level. It implies stability and symmetry. To be level, equally proportioned. To have order, composure. It implies equity and impartiality, uprightness, truth, honesty and justice, all of which lead to wisdom.

The terms of the Ayuuk language that name those virtues are '*tey*' or '*teyë*', meaning straight, honourable; '*tuknax*', meaning even; and '*kijpxy*' meaning levelled, the same that are ascribed to symmetry, equality, equity; likewise, the word '*teyë*' is intimately linked to the concept of *tey'yäjtën*, which refers to certainty, straightforwardness, justice, truth.

The opposite terms are '*ja key-ja pat*', meaning unbalanced; '*ja këjxm-ja nääxypy*', meaning uneven; '*wiity-kuuty*', meaning crooked; and '*ney-xëkety*', meaning twisted. Similarly, the concepts expressing the fact of not being well are '*yuu-pä'äm*' (illness), '*pëjkën-aato'onën*' (pains), '*jäjën-jëmu'umën*' (burning sensations), as well as '*ayo'on-jotmay*' (problems-misfortunes) and '*ayo'on-tsoytyu'un*' (problems-shame), the results of which lead to conditions of weakness, depression (*yäjk'ayow*), worry, anxiety (*mä'äyën-täjën*), sadness, and affliction (*mo'onën-tujkën*), which in turn create physical, emotional and spiritual frailty.

The relation of ääw-joot (word-heart) and joot-winmä'äny (heart-thought)

The *difrasismo aakujk'äj-jotkujk'äjtën* already implies the terms *ääw-joot* 'word and heart' and *joot-winmä'äny* 'heart and thought', where it originates. To be *aakujk-jotkujk* is 'to hold the word and the heart in precise vertical position', or to be consistent with what is said and felt and with what is felt and thought.

In these interrelated and consistent concepts, lie, manipulation and deceit, do not fit. Corruption, exploitation or harm done to some for the benefit of others are equally unconceivable.

Figure 56 Family giving an offering to the Ayuuk gods, on top of I'px Yuukm, to thank that the year he served the community, as an authority, there were no problems. Photo: Juan Carlos Reyes Gómez, 2012.

The link between oy-tsuj (what is good), tsuj-wä'äts (beauty), oy-jantsy (truth) and tsuj-yajkxon (what is right)

What is good is tightly related to what is beautiful, clean, right, certain and true; this is expressed through the following *difrasismos*: *oy-tsuj* (good-beautiful) 'what is right'; *tsuj-wä'äts* (beautiful-clean) 'what is beautiful'; *oy-jantsy* (good-certain) 'what is true'; and *tsuj-yajkxon* (beautiful-well done) 'what is right'. Hence, what is not right (*ko'oypyë*) is associated with what is filthy (*axëëkpë*), which in turn renders the idea of what is not beautiful, which is expressed through the *difrasismo* '*ko'oypyë-axëëkpë*', meaning what is bad, dirty, improper-what is not allowed.

Conclusions

The expression '*aakujk'äjt-jotkujk'äjtën*' implies an intimate relation between what is said and felt and between what is felt and thought. It also requires behaving with sincerity, speaking the truth, acting with honesty, as well as practising good virtues and values like humbleness, respect, tolerance, solidarity and readiness to help whoever suffers from some misfortune or lacks what is most essential. To be in balance and harmony is *to live really well*, going beyond the health-illness relation, be it physical or mental. Thus it also implies, to a great extent, spiritual matters. It is searching to be well with the *whole* in all fields and levels of our existence. Those who succeed in reaching balance and harmony also have attained symmetry, stability, plenitude and wisdom.

References

Campbell, L. & T. Kaufman. 1976. "A linguistic look at the Olmecs." *American Antiquity* 41(1): 80- 89. http://www.jstor.org/ stable/279044 (consulted 24 June 2015).

Clark, J. E. & M. Blake. 1989. "El origen de la civilización en Mesoamérica: los olmecas y mokaya del Soconusco de Chiapas, México." In *El Preclásico o formativo: Avances y perspectivas*, Carmona M. M., editor, México: Museo Nacional de Antropología.

Justeson J. & T. Kaufman. 1993. "A Decipherment of Epi-Olmec Hieroglyphic Writing." *Science* (New Series) 259(5102), 1703-1711.

Kaufman, T. & J. Justeson. 2001. *Epi-olmec Hieroglyphic Writing and Texts.* https://www.albany.edu/pdlma/EOTEXTS.pdf (Consulted 15 August 2015).

Pérez S. T. 2012. "La escritura istmeña o epiolmeca como antecedente de la maya: una revisión histórica." *Revista Digital Universitaria* 13 (11). http: //www.revista.unam.mx/vol.13/num11/art106/index.html (Consulted 5 June 2015).

Pohl, M. E. D. et al. 2002. "Olmec Origins of Mesoamerican Writing." *Science* 298, 1984-1987. www.sciencemag.org (Consulted 3 June 2015).

Pye, M. E. & J. E. Clark. 2006. "Los olmecas son Mixe-Zoques: Contribuciones de Gareth W. Lowe a la arqueología del formativo." In *XIX Simposio de Investiga-*

ciones Arqueológicas en Guatemala, 2005, Laporte J. P., B. Arroyo y H. Mejía, eds., 70-82, Guatemala: Museo Nacional de Arqueología y Etnología. www. asocia-ciontikal.com/pdf/07---Pye-y- Clark.05---Digital.pdf (Consulted 20 August 2015)

Reyes Gómez, J. C. 2017. *Tiempo, Cosmos y Religión del Pueblo Ayuuk*. Archaeological Studies Leiden University 37, the Netherlands: Leiden University Press. https:// openaccess.leidenuniv.nl/handle/1887/51102

Wichmann, S. et altera. 2008. "Posibles correlaciones lingüísticas y arqueológicas vinculadas con los olmecas." In *Olmeca. Balance y perspectivas. Memoria de la Primera Mesa Redonda*, Uriarte M. T. y R. B. González Lauck, eds., 667-683, México: Universidad Nacional Autónoma de México.

Notes

1 The Ayuuk (or Mixe) are an indigenous people of Mexico, inhabiting the state of Oaxaca, in the south of the country. Their territory is situated between the Gulf of Mexico and the Isthmus of Tehuantepec, extending over about 6,000 km2. These people consist of more than two hundred communities, mostly living in highland areas, mountainous and cold zones, around a sacred mountain called I'px Yuukm (The Place of the Twenty Mountains), one of the highest mountains of the state of Oaxaca, with a summit towering almost 3,500 metres above sea level. According to the national census, the Ayuuk population in 2015 numbered a little more than 140,000, of whom a little more than 130,000 speak the Ayuuk language, making it – of the fifteen indigenous languages spoken in the state – the fourth most spoken in Oaxaca, behind the Zapotec, Mixtec and Mazatec languages.

2 The terms '*aakujk'äjt-jotkujk'äjtën*' are composed of following vocables: *aa* (contracted form of *ääw*), 'word'; *kujk* 'in vertical position', and *-äjt* (verbalizer), and *jot* (contraction of *joot*), 'heart', *kujk* 'in vertical position'; *-äjt* (verbalizer), and *-ën* (nominalizer). Literally, it means 'to hold the word and the heart in vertical position'; in short, it means 'to be well', with 'well' being understood in the largest possible meaning of the word.

3 A glossary of religious Ayuuk terms, in Ayuuk and in Spanish, can be found in Reyes Gómez (2017).

Mentawai shamans in Indonesia: restoring threatened harmony

Reimar Schefold

Siberut is the northernmost and largest island – 4,030 square kilometres – of the Mentawai archipelago, which is located off the west coast of Sumatra.[1] The local kin groups (*uma*) on Siberut traditionally live in large longhouses, also called *uma*. In these communities, comprised on average of five to ten families, particular emphasis is placed on maintaining a harmonious balance. Central to this goal are the ideas about the soul. The Mentawaians believe that everything – people, animals, plants and objects – has a soul. People and their souls have to be in good relationship with each other. If through their behaviour the necessary consideration of their souls is disregarded, the souls might panic, flee far away and seek protection from the ancestors. Their owners must then die.

A lack of consideration for the soul means neglecting all that the soul expects from the human being: a beautiful lifestyle in everyday life with ornaments, tranquillity and good food, and, during ritual periods, festive dances and artistic performances. In the rituals, harmful influences, such as malignant spirits, are summoned and expelled from the *uma*. It is also necessary to respect taboos for the sake of the soul, refraining from specific acts that, for magical reasons, are considered incompatible with certain planned activities and thus might cause harm to people, their souls and their possessions. The Mentawaians often use analogous thinking to explain these rules. It is, for instance, taboo to eat anything sour while engaged in activities surrounding hunting. Sour and sharp are seen as equivalents. If one violated the taboo, they would likely injure themselves with 'sharp' weapons. Garden work offers another example; a newborn's father may not engage in any activity that could cause a plant to wither. If he did, he and especially his child would wither as well.

Each person is responsible for a good relationship with his soul. If something goes wrong, perhaps because a taboo has been disrespected, the disorder may manifest itself in illness. In order to restore the disturbed relationship and make the soul 'tame' (*maom*) again, a healing ritual is needed. In charge of its implementation are the shamans, the *kerei*.

In each *uma*, one or more of the men have the position of *kerei*. They have undergone a lengthy and elaborate initiation under the guidance of an experienced teacher (*paumat*). The candidate is not required to have a special psychic disposition. During the initiation, the shaman in training learns the relevant songs and incantations, and acquires knowledge of magical medicinal plants of which there exist many dozens. Their characteristic formal or other perceptible qualities are associated with desirable elements in the healing process. These qualities reveal something about the nature of the plants, which prove them to be suitable for

Figure 57 Shaman's headband (*sorot* or *luat*). A broad strip of split rattan is wrapped in fabric and decorated in a patterned arrangement with strings of glass beads. Added to the headband are decorated little rods that are placed behind the ears. Glass beads, *bebeget* rattan, cotton fabric, chicken feathers, vegetative material, mother-of pearl. Siberut, Mentawai, Indonesia, 1950. 20 × 19 × 30 cm. NMVW no. 7086-13. Photo: Irene de Groot.

conveying the concerns of the shamans to the instances that they want to act upon. For example, a plant with a corkscrew-like stalk is called 'twisting' (*pilok*); in line with its shape and its name, the soul of this plant is willing to follow corresponding incantations and ensure, for example, that harmful influences are 'twisted away'.

The special ability of shamans to communicate directly with souls and spirits is expressed in a gift that distinguishes them from their fellow villagers: they have 'seeing eyes' that can visibly perceive spirits and souls. The acquisition of this gift also occurs through the shamanic initiation and is the magical consequence of a strictly secret learning process. Shamans can observe what threatens a stray soul and, with the help of mediating plants, take appropriate countermeasures. They try to figure out where in the surrounding area the soul of a sick person got lost. There they lure the soul with flowers and ornaments and convince it to come back home. The actual healing ceremony is performed in the *uma*. The harmful influences are expelled, the patient is cleansed, and they and their soul are strengthened again.

In addition to their healing work, the shamans also have a preventive role. During the great periodic rituals of the group, the *uma* is purified of all the dangerous forces that want to nest there. The shamans can see the evil spirits and chase them away with glowing torches of protective magical plants (see fig. 58). At the height of

Figure 58 A "seeing" shaman expels harmful forces from the communal house during a nocturnal ritual in the Sakuddei uma. 1967. Photo Reimar Schefold.

Figure 59 Adorned shaman dancing with *abak ngalou* pendant, *toggoro* loincloth and *sabo* dancing apron. 1978. Photo Reimar Schefold.

the festival, the shamans, ringing small brass bells, call out the souls of individual *uma* members and exhort them not to wander far and wide. In order to attract them, everything that pleases the souls is intensified: ornaments and flowers are spread out, and the flesh of great sacrificial pigs is presented invitingly. Artistic expressions are also part of the calling: specially for the souls and ancestors, birds are made of wood, painted and hung at the entrance (see Schefold 2017, fig. 2). Inside, dances are performed the whole night long, which should also please the souls. At the end of the ritual, the *uma* is again prepared for everyday life.

The special position of the shaman is reflected in his equipment. During a long ritual (*pukereijat*) at the end of the initiation, attended by the entire community, the shaman receives the ornaments that are particular to his position: a headband (*sorot* or *luat*) made of a rattan strip wrapped in fabric and decorated with glass beads, woven fibre rings for his upper arms (*lekkau*), a necklace (*tudda*) of imported

Figure 60 Shaman's chest. Mentawai, Indonesia, ca. 1950. Wood, rotan. 17 × 65 × 16 cm. NMVW TM-5769-1. Photo: Irene de Groot.

ochre-tinted glass beads, a dance apron (*sabo*) of variously coloured pieces of fabric, and a red-dyed loincloth made of softened bark (*toggoro*). Two other ornaments are of great importance in the ceremonies as well: a pendant (*abak ngalou*) with amulets attached to it and a hair ornament (*jarajara*) made of feathers and the ribs of palm leaves, again with an amulet (see fig. 59). How these amulets are obtained is the secret of the *kerei*. They claim to have wrested some of them away from the ancestors, who appear as guests at the close of the consecration. The shaman keeps all of these paraphernalia in special small wooden cases (*salipa*; see fig. 60).

The shaman's wife (from now on called 'kerei' as well) will also wear a special ornament during rituals: the *teteku* crown (see fig. 61). She also wears a characteristically striped skirt (*sinaibak*) made of different strips of fabric sewn together. She does not participate actively in the healing ceremonies, but like her husband must observe certain taboos on these occasions. She complements him in conducting incantations during some of the ceremonies that take place at the large communal rituals. In rare instances, a trance state – a phenomenon that is the hallmark of all shamans – may also be entered into by a woman. Women who have this ability can sometimes exercise healing functions as well.

Figure 61 Shaman's wife, with festive *teteku* ornament. Mentawai, Indonesia, 1978. Photo Reimar Schefold.

People achieve the state of trance through specific dances and the sounds of rhythmic drumming. It is considered proof of a shaman's supernatural connections. Another sign and proof of such connections is the ability of some shamans to dance in fire. The ancestors see to it that no harm comes to him.

A desire for personal recognition might be one of the main motivations for becoming a shaman. A shaman often receives attention from neighbouring groups, and is invited to perform rituals for them. Shamans are allowed to break away from the norm and emerge as individuals in an otherwise egalitarian social structure. In some valleys, more than one-quarter of the adult men have this status, although maintaining it is difficult. They must abide by onerous taboos. Travelling to perform healing ceremonies in neighbouring *uma* constitutes an economic disruption. There is no substantial personal gain. The compensation for a shaman's services comes in the form of larger portions of the sacrificial meat of slaughtered animals, which upon his return to his *uma*, a shaman must as always share with all others present. In everyday life, the shaman takes on the ordinary tasks of every adult man.

During the twentieth century, most Mentawaians converted to Christianity. As a result, the shamanic traditions described here have only been preserved to some extent in the interior of Siberut. Nevertheless, the influence of the old ideas, especially with regard to the *kerei*, can still be felt everywhere. This also applies to the appearance of the shamans: while otherwise largely modern clothing prevails, they appear in their traditional outfits on festive occasions, for example, in healing ceremonies, to which they are still regularly drawn. This gives them renown even among young Mentawaians. The *kerei* are proud of their position and are currently tolerated by the government. Whether this will ensure the continued existence of their role for the future depends on the extent shamanism is cherished by the young generation as part of their Mentawaian identity.

References

Schefold, R. 2017. *Toys for the Souls. Life and Art on the Mentawai Islands*. Bornival: Primedia sprl.

Schefold, R. 2019. "Shamans in Siberut, Mentawai. Restoring threatened harmony." In: Steven G. Alpert (ed.): *Artoftheancestors.com, May 27*.

Notes

1   An earlier version of this article has been published in Schefold (2019).

Life Itself is a Polyrhythm – On Healing

Maria van Daalen

Prologue

Healing – what exactly is healing? An old practice, of helping others in distress, that has likely been around since the beginning of times. Meaning that its origins could very well date from before we had a language in which fiction is possible and metaphors and the structuring of time and memory.[1]

Other animals are known to recognize distress in living creatures and to try to help. But the human language that developed in us and through us made it possible to have a discourse with everyone and everything around us, to understand the stories of clients and the history of a disease, and to accumulate knowledge and transfer it to the next generations, orally and written, combined with rituals.

Healing is not only listening to and understanding what is said. Healing is about compassion. From pain to full recovery, the body heals and the soul can heal too. The process of renewal begins with acknowledgement of the suffering.

Fear of death being the ultimate fear, the mystery religions aim to heal us from this first. New initiates experience a ritual of 'death' and 'rebirth', with a time of absence from society, followed by being 'reborn' and receiving a new name. A ritual

Figure 62 In my *badji* or altar-room are altars for several groups of *Lwa-yo* ('angels' or 'mysteries' in Haitian Vodou): white for Rada, red for Petro, golden for Papa Loko and Legba (corner), purple for Ghede (floor). I serve the *Lwa* with drinks, food, lighted candles, flowers, songs, etc. On the floor a special *sevis* (service) for Papa Ogou, with two machetes. Interesting, in this photo also a service for a *keris pusaka* (floor). This is not Haitian Vodou but part of the Indonesian tradition. The Dutch-Indonesian connection has its roots in colonial times. 2020. Photo: Maria van Daalen.

Figure 63 An oil lamp is made for a certain *Lwa*. This *lamp* is for Manbo Erzulie Freda, to help a client in a love situation. Ingredients can be olive oil, pink rose petals, perfume, certain herbs (in the oil), and of course a wick. Once the *lamp* is lighted, it has to burn continuously for a certain amount of days. 2020. Photo: Maria van Daalen.

Figure 64 This *vévé* is made by Maria van Daalen. A *vévé* is traced in cornflour and is a portal for a certain *Lwa* ('angel' or 'mystery' in Haitian Vodou). There are many different *vévé*'s. This one is for Legba who 'opens the door'. Added to it are three stars, a design with two crossed v's, and the candle and mug (in cornflour). All designs are traditional. The *vévé* is activated with a lighted candle, with food (sugarcane e.o.), with drinks, and with certain songs. The eight shawls or *mouswa* in seven colors plus white, symbolize all the *Lwa*. 2020. Photo: Maria van Daalen.

bath ('baptism') is often part of the proceedings.[2] Ritual baths can be a part of a healer's treatment too, washing off the bad past and making people new.

Healers are found in all times and amongst all peoples. A healer is a compassionate human being who has ample knowledge of the traditional healing of a certain culture, often enhanced by the knowledge of healing traditions of other, connected cultures. She is at ease with herself, works with spirits, ancestral or from other abodes,[3] uses divinatory means (cards, bones, shells, etc.), has been initiated in a certain tradition and by its ethics and moral guidelines chooses her path, may use drums and other musical instruments, and songs, dances, colors (clothing), perfumes, herbs and the many other materials that nature provides, and is not afraid to speak up for her tradition and culture.

Much of what I say here about the healer is optional, not demanded; most religions and traditions have their own *regleman* (in Haitian Vodou, the rules by which we live and work). We know our roots, we honor and respect[4] our traditions and cultures, and we are continuously being taught by our spiritual family, our ancestors and our spirits, by herbs, dreams and experiences, by clients and by the diseases themselves.

Manbo Travay

A Vodou priestess and her spiritual work

'God, the Ancestors, and the *Lwa*',[5] we say in Haitian Vodou when we name our spiritual helpers. To God we pray. The ancestors, and our *Lwa*, we address, with prayers, songs, gifts, and we ask for help and advice. You don't need an initiation for *sevi Lwa*, to serve the *Lwa*. But the initiations, with their different levels, open up your soul for a better communication with the spirits – not only with your Vodou spirits but also, often, with many other spiritual beings.

Your person is hereto a vital 'point' in time and space. The body is the altar. Every experience is part of that. It translates as compassion in your *travay*, or, healer's work, when you've gone yourselves through the tribulations and hardships that your clients face who come to you for help. When you yourself have worked your way out of the stress, the hurt, the pain, the depression, and found a way to harness your emotions – your fear, your anger, your distrust of others, your sadness, your terrible shock – in becoming whole again, but now newly armed with the power of those emotions: you have found and built, in yourself, the strength of the healer.[6] When Jesus says, 'Physician, heal thyself', this is what is meant.[7]

As we all have different experiences, all of us have different expertise. You may be asked to treat illnesses of the soul, the mind, the body; your help is needed in situations of love, work, money, in looking for a new home, or in family relations and

Figure 65 *Agwe* by Pierrot Barra (1942-1999). Agwe is a *Lwa* (spirit) from the sea, depicted as an admiral or captain of the ship Imamou which is taking the dead to their ancestral homes. Haïti. Plastic dolls, fabrics, various materials, 63,5 x 110 x 117 cm. NMVW no. AM-681-14. Photo: Ferry Herrebrugh.

Figure 66 *Agwe* (part of the installation *Le Monde des Ambaglos – The World of the Underwater Beings* which consists of three *Lwa* in three boats: Mambo Inan, Agwe and Erzulie) by Edouard Duval-Carrié, Haïti, 2007-08. Polyester, various materials, 255 x 95 x 300 cm (boat; incl. the long arms of Agwe 500 cm). NMVW no. AM-681-2a.

in contact with the ancestors. Oftentimes you will find yourself patiently guiding a client away from certain habits, knowing far too well that he will continue to harm himself if he doesn't learn to make changes, however small.

Two simple rules of healing

True magic is a healer's tool, but it's not like waving a magic wand and we're done. Changing course a little bit and staying on that path for a long time makes for a different future. Much like loosing weight, or directing a ship to a distant destination. Sailing out from Iceland slightly more southwest than usual, doesn't mean much as long as the same coastline shimmers behind you, but keep at it and you'll end up in L'Anse aux Meadows, Canada, instead of in Greenland, Denmark, as the Vikings

Figure 67 *L' anniversaire de Damballah* (*Damballah's Birthday*) by Préfète Duffaut, 2007, Haïti. Damballah is a *Lwa* of wisdom and healing. Painting on canvas, 103 x 103 cm. NMVW no. AM-681-8. Photo: Irene de Groot.

found out. No wonder we have Mèt Agwé,[8] the Captain, as an important spirit to help us steer the right course in life.

My motto as a healer is 'Empower the client'. To have the clients participate actively helps the healing process. My work and their work together forge the magic.

The client's part is often seemingly 'just magical' and not 'logically' related to the problem. But this way we shift the focus, and the energy, we open a door and the movement of change gains momentum.

'Go every Sunday to the Roman Catholic church in town to hear Mass. Go on foot': be active and learn to have faith. A religion is a belief system. Its rituals convey meaning. 'Always give a beggar some money and ask him to pray for you': show respect and understand the essence of asking and receiving. 'Wear this color on that weekday, avoid wearing black': there is power in color. 'Collect some dust from the entrance of three different banks': understand the notion of place. 'Leave this magic object which I've made specifically to help with the problem, in such and such a place and keep it there for such and such a time': learn to trust. 'Put a request in handwriting under a candle, light it on a certain weekday and let it burn out...'[9]

And I'll seal the entrances of the house with prayers, songs, light and libations, so the good comes in and the bad stays out.

Balance

An important word in the practice of Haitian Vodou is 'balanse' ('bah-lahn-SAY', Haitian Kreyol). We bring back the balance in the lives of our clients, we balance them. A basic ritual, called a *salute*, shows this.

I light a white candle and pray over it. I take that candle and an enamel mug filled with fresh water in my left hand, and my *asson* in my right, and I salute the four directions, in the sequence East, West, North, South, holding up all items while singing a *Lwa* song. I then make a libation for the spirits by pouring a few drops on the ground left, right, middle.[10]

With the salute, which is like a dance, I make the crossroads: since time immemorial the place where this reality and the spirit world are in contact and merge. I am in the centre. My body is an altar. It is the pillar that connects this world and the other world[s]. I pour the libation. Then I can put a question to the spirits in the Other World.

A treatment is tailormade

And when I do, an answer will come. Once one of my three brothers was very tired and called on me for help. 'Let me dream on it', I said. In the dream, Mèt Agwé came to me and showed me how to make a tincture of the leaves of the *Thuja occidentalis* in my garden. I had never heard of such a thing. These aren't trees from the Caribbean. But the *Lwa* work with what's available.

The tincture had a strong and beautiful forest fragrance. I tried it myself first and slept well. So did my brother! I told him to use it on his head and shoulders, but not to swallow a single drop, as it contains thujone, which is poisonous. My sister-in-law asked me if she could use it too, but no: for her a floral scent is best.

Before I was made a Manbo I never made herb baths, tinctures, ointments, but now I have many, with recipes from my *Lwa*...

Epilogue

Life is a polyrhythm. As is Haitian Vodou drumming in the temple during a ritual. The *Lwa* surface in my poetry, the *Lwa* are present through my *vévés*, which are the ritual drawings I make with corn flour on the floor, the *Lwa* dance with me in the altar room and talk to me in the garden. Or in dreams. The essence of healing is joy.

Notes

1   Mnemosyne, Memory, is the mother of the Muses. I'd like to refer the reader here to Julian Jaynes's *The Origin of Consciousness in the Breakdown of the Bicameral Mind* (1976) and Yuval Noah Harari's *Sapiens: A Brief History of Humankind* (2011).

2   In Christianity I see many parallels with the Mysteries of Demeter, of Dionysus, and other so-called 'mystery religions'. Formerly, Christian converts were baptized at Easter and given a new name, after having spent a night in seclusion and in prayer. I view the initiation in Haitian Vodou called a *Kanzo*, as essentially a mystery religion's experience.

3   Spirits can be present in nature (rocks, trees, herbs, etc.) and/or in the Land of Ginen (Vodou *Lwa*), or still elsewhere. Note: Seeing and/or hearing spirits is often characterized academically, for example in psychology and psychiatry, as having visual and/or auditory 'hallucinations'. However, these are normal and relatively common experiences. See also Jaynes (1976). I myself don't experience a dichotomy between being a Manbo and having a university education (drs./ MA). 'Cognitive dissonance' doesn't quite cover it.

4   'Honè / respè', 'honor / respect', is a traditional Haitian Kreyol call and response greeting.

5   A *Lwa*, also Loa, is a Haitian Vodou spirit, i.e. a spiritual being on the level of an angel or archangel.

6   I myself have been raped. Yes, # metoo. But coming from that horrid experience and becoming a *Manbo Asogwe* (a Haitian Vodou priestess) in 2007, while I was steadfastly walking on the path of healing, has made me a healer of clients who have been deeply wounded by similar experiences, such as women who are victims of human trafficking and forced prostitution.

7   I.e. do this first before you try to heal anybody else. Luke 4:23 (Bible, King James Version).

8   Mèt Agwé is the exemplary Captain who steers the Ship and knows the Way when no way can be seen, as is the case on the surface of the ocean. All Vodou *Lwa* have their own way of handling things and will show up with a clear purpose.

9   These are all examples and only parts of prescriptions. None of these should be done without proper guidance by a *Manbo* or *Houngan* (priest in Haitian Vodou).

10   Again: there's more to it. Some remarks. An *asson* is a ritual object. It consists of a dried calabash with a natural handle, emptied of seeds, covered with a net with beads and sometimes snake vertebrae (old assons). Attached to it is a Roman Catholic altar bell. As small as it is, it reminds us of the three historical roots of Haitian Vodou: Taíno Indian, [West]African, European.

White enamel mugs and bowls (for baths) are found in all temples. They may have been in use since the early nineteenth century. The beautiful white Vodou dresses with long skirts and ballooning sleeves may also be from that time. Haiti, at the time called Saint Domingue, was a French colony. The anti-slavery insurrection and the revolution (1791-1804) made it a free country, called Haiti ('ayiti', 'mountainous' in Taíno).

5 Global interactions

Cunera Buijs and Wouter Welling

The exchange and relocation of cultural traditions are not new phenomena. From centuries of trade around the world new elements emerged and foreign components were incorporated into presumed homogeneous cultures. In the sixteenth, seventeenth and eighteenth centuries, slavery was one of the major factors causing spiritual traditions to move. Enslaved peoples with African origins were shipped from their home countries to the New World and brought their traditions with them. These spiritual activities were forbidden and suppressed by plantation owners, colonizers and missionaries. However, the people forced into slavery succeeded in keeping and hiding part of their traditions, and created new religions using elements of Christianity. The spiritual fusion resulted in African diaspora religions (Hübner and Welling 2009).

In the present day, global interactions continue to take place and spiritual traditions from different parts of the world continue to be incorporated into new forms of spirituality. This is a worldwide phenomenon, occurring not only in the Netherlands but in many parts of the world. In the Netherlands and Peru, for example, Sebastiaan van 't Holt investigated changes in ayahuasca traditions. He witnessed tourists from Europe and America now travelling to the Amazon as 'consumers of native spirituality' in a quest for healing, balance and relief of traumatic experiences. Shipibo shamans (*curanderos*) treat foreigners in local villages and in ayahuasca centres in larger cities, but are accused by others in the Shipibo community of being 'Disney shamans', changing practices on demand and performing for the consumer public.

Figure 68 *The Last Supper* by Frantz Augustin Zéphirin. The twelve apostles surrounded by *Lwa* (spirits) from the vodou pantheon. Haïti, 2001. Acrylic on canvas, 76 x 101 cm. NMVW no. AM-670-2. Photo: Ferry Herrebrugh.

Young people in the West are looking for a spiritual, individual experience rather than a dogmatic and collective religious one. Many are attracted to neo-paganism and New Age spiritual practices. Healing festivals have become increasingly popular. One way that balance and harmony, as well as self-expression, are articulated is through psychedelic trance or 'psytrance', a music trend dating from the 1990s, popular today in the Dutch neo-hippy scene. Iris Hesse conducted research among the Rotoris, young organizers of such festivals in the Netherlands. She compares the role of the DJ, as a leader of the music event, with that of the shaman in facilitating a state of trance during a healing ritual. Hesse (this chapter) argues that music and dance have healing power: 'the psytrance community is a surrounding for social healing and can improve the lives of young people'.

The worlds of ritual specialists and visual artists also intermingle. Artists like Beuys and Abramović use(d) contemporary art for individual and community transformations and healing, showing an affinity with spiritual shamanic traditions.

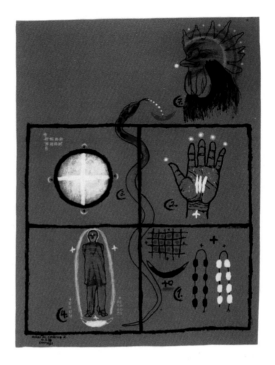

Figure 69 *Cosas del espiritu 2* by Santiago Rodríguez Olazábal, 1998. In an early age the artist was initiated in the Oshún cult; he is a Santería/Regla de Ifa priest. His work is strongly related to this African diaspora religion. Cuba. Mixed techniques on paper, 88 x 67 cm. NMVW no. AM-606-18. Photo: Ferry Herrebrugh.

Spiritual ways of thinking are based on abstraction, association and symbolism. Healing, fear, hope and spirituality are connected to inspirited materials and colours. Wouter Welling, curator of contemporary art (this chapter), explains that the Dutch artist Remy Jungerman developed an imagery that connects Surinamese Winti rituals and Marron symbolism to the European modernism of Mondrian. Similarly, the Cuban artist Santiago Rodriguez Olazábal, who is also a priest in the Cuban Regla de Ifá religion, which has African roots, uses symbols like the cross in his installations to speak across art and spirituality. One of these is a Congolese cosmogramme, in which the stages of life are represented (fig. 69). Artists are familiar with this visual language and often relate art to the other world, exploring the space between the visible and the invisible.

References
Hübner, I. and W. Welling, 2009. *Roots & More – the journey of the spirits.* Berg en
    Dal: Afrika Museum.

Transforming traditions: ayahuasca in the Netherlands and Peru

Sebastiaan van 't Holt

In 2017, as a student of cultural anthropology at the university of Leiden, the Netherlands, I was invited by the Dutch Museum Volkenkunde in Leiden, where I held an internship, to attend the yearly Gerbrands lecture. On the evening of the conference, the museum officially presented me with a grant to support my research on ayahuasca practices in the Netherlands and Peru. My research would ultimately contribute to the Healing Power exhibition, which opened in the summer of 2019 in the Museum Volkenkunde.

In 2018 I spent two months with Shipibo shamans in the Peruvian Amazon. The vast Amazon rainforest is home to more than forty thousand plant species, making it the place with the highest biodiversity on earth. The Shipibo community consists of about thirty-five thousand people living in about three hundred villages in the Pucallpa and Loreto areas in Peru. The Shipibo have great knowledge of the tropical rainforest and its ecosystem. They know which plants are edible and which can be used for medicinal purposes; some of this knowledge is protected and secret. All plants have their own spirits to whom offerings are made. Outside of Peru, ayahuasca is the best known, but the tobacco plant is sacred as well and of similar ritual importance. Other Amazonian plants used in Western medicine are cat's claw, cinchona, curare, and jaborandi.

Shipibo shamans administer different plants, often in combination, to their clients with the aim of learning and healing. From all over the world people travel to the Amazon in order to follow a diet, guided by a shaman, of specific plants or shamanic rituals. They may either seek out an adventure for themselves or partake in organized, sometimes extensive programmes with flower baths and massages.

Here I focus on ayahuasca, an Amazonian brew made out of two plants: the ayahuasca vine and the chacruna leaf. Among the Shipibo, the brew is usually drunk in a night-time ceremony, led by an indigenous *curandero* (healer) or shaman. Ayahuasca is perceived as a holy plant, an 'intellectual master' with specific characteristics. The word 'ayahuasca' stems from an indigenous South American language, and means 'vine of the soul'. Drinking ayahuasca brings people into a kind of dream state. People may vomit after ingesting ayahuasca; this is seen as a cleansing of body and mind, and part of the healing process.

For hundreds of years different peoples of the Amazon have been drinking the brew together. Ceremonies are held in order to strengthen bonds within families, to interact with the natural environment and to get into contact with ancestors. Drinking ayahuasca opens the door to a spiritual realm. Animals, plants, mythical figures, unknown creatures and complex geometrical patterns appear. (Such patterns are often reflected in Shipibo textiles and pottery.) Ancestors or living relatives manifest their presence, either in their human form or in a slightly different one. Generally understood as spirits by the users of ayahuasca, these entities are able to communicate with those partaking in the ceremony, either visually or through other senses (hearing, feeling, smelling). Ayahuasca churches such as the Santo Daime are spreading across the globe. In The Hague and Amsterdam for example, members of the church come together for complex ceremonies, drinking ayahuasca as a holy sacrament and singing hymns. These are organized often under the guidance of Dutch ritual specialists, themselves educated by indigenous *curanderos*. This is not without juridical problems. The hallucinogenic molecule dimethyltryptamine (DMT), part of the ayahuasca drink, is illegal in the Netherlands. It is considered dangerous for people who are already in an unstable state of mind.

Ayahuasca's increasing popularity in the Netherlands raises different questions. There are concerns about the safety of the 'trip tea', but the reality of shamanism is questioned as well. *Does it really work?* There is also a sceptical attitude towards the method of shamans. *Isn't it quackery?* I think that such questions are the result of

Figure 70 Diogenes Garcia amidst the chacruna plant. On his shirt is the image of the plant's leaf, together with the head of a serpent and a cross-section of the ayahuasca vine. Above that is a rectangle of patterns, as they are observed in ayahuasca visions. His corona (hat) is now part of the museum's collection. Peru, 2018. Photo: Sebastiaan van 't Holt.

ignorance regarding different cultural systems, and are mostly asked by those who have never been in contact with a shaman.

There is another question, predominantly asked by people who are familiar with shamanism, that deals with the differences between shamans. Which shamans are real, and which are not? During my ayahuasca research, I heard people refer to 'Disney shamanism', a phrase that implies that it's just an act, a trick, a fairy tale. Usually this phrase was used in relation to shamanism in Peru, not in the Netherlands. This may be due in part to the expectations people have, and how these differ from reality. In Peru, many may expect that they can get the 'real deal' from indigenous healers, and are critical if they perceive something to be inauthentic. In the Netherlands, in a Dutch context, ritual specialists are just considered to be 'better' or 'lesser' capable in their work; the question of authenticity is moot.

So, what do we expect, rightly or wrongly so, of shamanism in the Amazon? First of all there are misunderstandings about shamans themselves. Shamanism may pass from father to son, or a person may be selected as a 'chosen one' by a sign from the Otherworld, or certain talents may be developed in the community. But one could also, for instance, decide to become a shaman out of financial considerations. Or one

Figure 71 Every morning Mama Rosa prepares different mixtures of plants. I asked a collaborator of the ayahuasca centre if he drinks it. He answers: 'No, I enjoy my sleep more lately'. Peru, 2018. Photo: Sebastiaan van 't Holt.

Figure 72 Shaman's costume (*Kushma*). Luis Marquez wore this costume while he was leading ayahuasca ceremonies. The serpent transfers his wisdom to the ceramic bowl that will contain that knowledge for the Shipibo culture. During ayahuasca ceremonies Luis Marquez has visions. He communicates these visions with his wife. Based on his stories she has created this cotton costume in six months' time. Luis Marquez explains: "Left you can see a *tinaja*, related to the festivities of the Shipibo and purple coloured chacruna leaves that give me life. Ayahuasca enables us to maintain our culture in spite of all the problems that we as Shipibo encounter. On the right a green anaconda is depicted who provides me wisdom, also about establishing a school for the Shipibo children." Peru, Pucallpa, Shipibo, 2018. NMVW no. 7163-1. Photo: Irene de Groot.

might be inspired by a neighbour or become a shaman after a healer successfully treated a son or daughter.

A 'rite of passage' does not necessarily take place. There are examples of people who decide to become a shaman at forty, and who only work with tourists, never in their practice meeting a Peruvian. Furthermore, there are Europeans and Americans who, after participating in many ceremonies, decide to stay in the Amazon and do shamanistic work there.

According to Kraemer in Adelaars et all. (1997, 142) the origin of ayahuasca might go back as far as twenty-five thousand years ago; it has certainly been used for a long time in the Amazon. 'Commercial ayahuasca shamanism', as Kraemer (1997) calls it, came into existence about two hundred years ago, through the trade with people from the Andes mountains. Shamans have thus long offered their services to people who are not part of their own indigenous group. From the sixteenth century onwards, during Spanish rule, parts of the Amazon became more accessible. As a result, many

Figure 73 Medical plant (*Llanten*) by Dimas Paredes Armas. Children's bronchitis is treated with *Llanten*. This is one of the plants the Shipibo find in their backyards or in the surrounding forests. Gouache, 32,5 x 38,5 cm. Peru, Pucallpa, Shipibo. 2011. NMVW no. 7163-6c). Photo: Irene de Groot.

groups became familiar with ayahuasca practices and started to integrate them into their own cultural traditions. More recently, influenced by the growing number of foreigners visiting the Amazon, ayahuasca shamanism found new forms again, with scientists trying to investigate ayahuasca's therapeutic value.

The worldwide interest in ayahuasca emphasizes the individual, healing aspect of the brew, but it was used earlier for other purposes as well. Anthropologist Jeremy Narby, author of a famous study on the subject, *The cosmic serpent: DNA and the origins of knowledge* (1998), compares ayahuasca to television: in the same way we might watch a show together, after a ceremony, the Shipibo share their stories and experiences. One of its functions is to create connectedness. Others describe ayahuasca as a practical tool, and according to some tales ayahuasca was used in earlier times for long-distance communication with people.

Ayahuasca shamanism is a practice par excellence through which the notion of 'healing' finds new forms. Claude Lévi-Strauss (1977) explains shamanic healing as

Figure 74 Shaman Antonio Vasquez postures with his pipe in front of the *maloka* (ceremonial space). Peru; 2018. Photo: Miriam Moreno.

a complex system of symbols presented by the healer, usually through singing, to the patient in order to help them cope with physical problems. Familiar with the cultural context, the patient can apprehend the symbols and use them as tools to transform illness. In this reading, there exists a magical relationship between the spoken word and reality.

In the current era, the common knowledge of these symbols is disappearing, as are the shamans with their extensive knowledge of the plants that surround them and the complex system of symbols. Although the concept of authenticity plays a part, that notion is used in many ways. The shaman now offers his services on the international market and together with the visitor creates a new reality based on their individual histories.

Issues related to tourism, cultural difference, financial exchange and 'realness' can play a role during a tourist's stay with a shaman. Context is important, but commodified spirituality still is spirituality, full of meaning, with beautiful aspects as well as dark sides. Committed people can use the experience for transformation, both for education and healing. In the end, I don't argue that shamanism, as influenced by tourism, is getting more superficial – not in all the meanings of the word, anyway. In my opinion, the shamanic reality transcends the personal, and maybe even the cultural, level. When properly guided, it can provide tools for solutions in our daily lives, allowing us to gain self-knowledge, stimulate creativity and experience healing.

References

Adelaars, Arno, Christian Rätsch and Claudia Müller-Ebeling. 2016. *Rituals, Potions and Visionary Art from the Amazon*. Studio City, CA: Divine Arts.

Lévi-Strauss, Claude. 1949. "L´Éfficacité symbolique." *Revue de L´Histoire des Religions*. Vol. 135, No. 1, 5-27. Paris: Libraire Plon.

Lévi-Strauss, Claude 1977. "The Effectiveness of Symbols." In: *Structural Anthropology*, Harmondsworth: Penguin books.

Narby, Jeremy. 1999. *The Cosmic Serpent, DNA and the Origins of Knowledge*. New York: Tarcher/Putnam.

Healing music: psychedelic trance and the search for balance

Iris Hesse

Psychedelic trance (psytrance) is a music genre that became popular in the 1990s in Western Europe but has since gradually moved to the background. Not generally known to the wider public, this genre is mainly popular among young people, and finds an audience today in the Netherlands and in other European countries. At the same time, 'green' or ecological concerns have grown and a neo-hippie movement has developed, both of which show remarkable similarities with the psytrance subculture. The neo-hippie movement arises from the deeply felt need to deal with the stressfulness of Western society and its rapid technological change. Young people experience pressure from the great variety of choices that they face in the individualizing and globalizing achievement-oriented society. Many are searching for rest and striving for a renewed connection with nature. There is an increasing interest in yoga, mindfulness, healthy food and fair-trade purchasing, including organic clothing. In addition, shamanism and other alternative healing methods are growing in popularity in Western society today. How recent societal changes are addressed in the psytrance scene, and vice versa, combined with the presumed healing power of psytrance music and dance will be explored in this article.

While studying cultural anthropology at the University of Leiden, the psytrance community caught my attention. In 2018, I decided to start a three-month research project, and made a film about a recently established organization in Rotterdam, the 'Rotoris', a group of young people who organize psytrance activities. Psytrance can be characterized as 'complex layered melodies that are composed of a bass line, a four-four-time kick, synthesizers, spatial melodic sounds and a tempo generally typically ranging from 140 to 160 BPM [beats per minute]' (Giorgia Gaia 2015, 2). In this article, I discuss the meaning of this subculture based on my interviews with Rotoris members.

Beginning in the 1960s, Western hippies travelled to Arjuna, India, and settled on the beach there. In the 1990s, this community began to produce and listen to a new genre of music, which they called 'psytrance'. Psytrance is thus not only a style of music but also a subculture, composed of a variety of practices, ideologies and spiritualities, and includes the use of 'drugs, dance, textile fashion, piercings, hair styling, tattooing, alternative diets, etc.' (Graham St John 2010, 4). These elements give the psytrance scene a particular character, and include the aims of renewing our relationship with ourselves and being in balance with nature, but without losing our connection with new technology and a modern standard of living.

Shamanism and spirituality in psytrance

Scott Hutson (1999) discovered during his research that 'ravers' (feasting dancers, originally street language from the Caribbean) feel that they have spiritual experiences while being at a rave. Based on testimonials of the rave experience, Hutson analyses rave as a form of healing; he writes, 'references to shamanism and catch-phrases about self-empowerment and spiritual healing permeate raver discourse and invite an anthropological perspective similar to that applied to non-biomedical healing in small scale, nonwestern societies' (Hutson 1999, 54). Being in the world, or making a new connection, can be achieved by dance and music. Or it can be achieved in a different way, through altered states of consciousness, which bring spiritual ease to people facing difficulties living in a rapidly changing society, which is experienced as 'uncertain'.

Robin Sylvan (2002, 13) takes these arguments further, stating that 'as a religious and cultural phenomenon, popular music has already precipitated the end of centuries of (Western) dominance of the mind-body split'. Relief from this mind-body split is achieved by the trance and dance practices that occur on the psytrance dance floor. Charles De Ledesma (2012, 35) explains that the volume of the bass, lights, decorations and choice of venue have an impact on the way partygoers understand 'the body, self, sociality and life expectation'. The embodied experience at psytrance parties is a mix of this all, where people often feel as there is room for individual and collective transformation (Maria Pini, 2001; see also Steven Van Wolputte 2004, 251). During my research, psytrance listeners expressed similar thoughts, suggesting that the embodied experience is channelled into a feeling of security, acceptance and safeness. For example, one person said:

> Yes, I often feel very much at home [at psy parties]. So I discovered a kind of home that I did not know in the past that I could have had. Precisely because you are accepted and welcomed. And there is such a relaxed atmosphere. And there is a possibility for self-expression. Actually, when I step into the location, I immediately feel relaxed. Like if you come home from a cold winter day and you sit in a warm bath, that kind of feeling. (Informant P6)

A shamanic state of being?

These feelings are rooted in the atmosphere on the dance floor and its surroundings. Through electronic dance music, like techno and psytrance, a similar effect can be reached to the altered state of consciousness achieved in shamanism. While dancing, ravers try to set aside their problems and thoughts and make their head empty. Drugs intensify this process. Ravers state that the use of drugs can create an alternative and more spiritual experience. Karenza Moore and Steven Miles (2004, 521) write that this is not an escape from real life, but a 'counter balance to it', and argue that 'much like other forms of consumption, young people's use of drugs is less about exploring the unpredictability of risk, and more about them actively maintaining a sense of stability in their everyday lives' (ibid. 506).

The major difference between shamanic forms of altered state of consciousness and trance arousal via music is that individuals create this state of mind themselves, instead of through the involvement of a shaman. There are, however, scholars who have a different opinion. Hutson (2000: 40) sees the DJ as a shaman who guides dancers to and through this state, functioning as 'harmonic navigator'. '"Techno-shamanism" can alter and manage the dancer's mood and mind', Hutson (ibid.) finds. There is something to be said for that, as the DJs, like shamans, create connections between the patient's body, society, and the spirit world (Homayun Sidky 2009; Geoffrey Samuel 1995, 256). Furthermore, it is generally known that music is capable of having 'psychical impact' on listeners and can modify the 'structure of consciousness' (Gilbert Rouget 1985, 120-23). On the psytrance dance floor, this manifests as dealing with emotions and searching for and acceptance of oneself, which are typical of the processes that young adolescents go through to become who they want to be in life. This therapeutic aspect was quite explicit in what the respondent above told me:

> You remove yourself from your everyday thoughts and activities so that you can create space in your head, yes, in fact what you are doing there, you let deeper layers of your subconscious come up. And through this, you get certain insights

Figure 75 Psy-fi Festival in Leeuwarden, the Netherlands. Shamanic elements can be seen during the festival and the clothing of the festival goers is inspired by non-Western cultures. The participants listen and react in their own way to the DJ and the music. 2018. Photo: Iris Hesse.

into yourself. And in this way it is a kind of therapy. I notice that when I'm on the dance floor. I can really enjoy the music, but at the same time I can also try self-therapy. I can let certain emotions come up and process them. You can accept everything that comes into your mind much better and you can process them much better, because you are already experiencing a good energy with many people around you who are all feeling the same energy. That is why it is a safe environment to practise self-reflection. (Informant P6)

Psytrance and New Age

'New Age' refers to spiritual and religious practices that developed in the 1970s in Western Europe. Social scientists emphasize the relationship between New Age and neo-shamanism. Neo-shamanism can be described as a 'set of notions and techniques that originated in the non-Western tribal societies and, within the framework of New Age spirituality, were adapted for the life of contemporary urban dwellers' (Galina Lindquist 1997, abstract). Furthermore, neo-shamanic practices are built on consciousness-altering techniques, 'when the Self is

Figure 76 Another way to reach a meditative state of mind is to make string-art. This image shows the result of one of the Rotoris workshops. This art decorates the psytrance festivals to enhance the experience of the visitors. 2018. Photo: Iris Hesse.

perceived to leave the body, to journey in other realities and to interact with the spiritual beings, enlisting their help for social, psychological, and physical healing' (ibid.). This combination of healing factors can contribute to personal and communal empowerment (Robert Wallis 2000). Psytrance listeners express agreement with this theory by stating that social, psychological, and physical healing and empowerment originates in the experience. For example, another participant in the research told me:

> Psytrance is life for me. It is a way for me to bring my own character and my vision into the world by making it myself. But it is also a way of the feasts and festivals, dancing and working with music and with other people that is, an experience. It is so much more than a form of entertainment alone. It heals you (Informant P4).

The technological aspect of the psytrance culture is also important for New Age shamanism. As Psyence Vedava (2015, 170) argues, the performative process happening on the dance floor of a psytrance event can be explained as '"technognosis":

Figure 77 Psy-fi Festival in Leeuwarden, the Netherlands. The community gathers at a heavily decorated stage. Nature elements prevail; at the centre is a world tree (axis mundi), which is symbolic of nature (Mother Earth). Their outfits are loose fitting, comfortable organic clothing that allow the participants to dance freely and let themselves go. Sometimes their wardrobes are inspired by non-Western cultures. High quality speakers are proportionally and efficiently placed to disperse the rhythmic beats and hypnotizing waves over the gathered public. In a sense, these elements can create a state of trance, which can linger on and enable people to dance for hours on end. 2018. Photo: Iris Hesse.

a concept that combines media, arts, performance and technology within the notion of gnosis'. According to Vedava (ibid.), technognosis 'affects participation and invites its multi-media and performance expression, triggering fundamental changes in ways of human thinking, imagining and operating: potentiating the adoption of participation as the next paradigm in human existence'. The participants in my research especially mentioned the healing effects on the body and mind from dancing at a psytrance event, due to the impressive sound system, light show and (digital) artwork. It is not necessarily that psytrance participants want to go back to a primitive way of life. Instead, they embrace modern technology in the search for balance between a modern lifestyle, nature and the self.

The healing power of music

In Western culture, youngsters and adolescents who struggle with daily life and those who are searching for identity and healing may find answers and solutions as part of psytrance communities. However, the psychosocial aspects of 'self-shamanizing' are also criticized. Desmond Thomas Tramacchi (2006, 29) found that modern subjects become 'their own clients and their own healers'. When people try to heal themselves without the guidance of a shaman or psychologist, this might go wrong. Graham St John (2018, 62) describes this process as 'seeking remedies for "alienation"

Figure 78 The film recordings made by Iris Hesse in the exhibition Healing Power in Leiden, 2019. On the right the sculpture *Princess of Trance* by the Belgian artist Bart van Dijck.

and "soul loss" compatible with desired liberation from dependence on biomedical solutions'. Loosening control over the mind is integral to this process of healing. This is experienced as difficult, because independence and self-responsibility are highly valued norms in Western culture, and ceding control to another is potentially troublesome (St John 2018). It is therefore important to pay close attention to a person's state of mind. People can become experienced in letting go of stressful feelings or finding a way to deal with the tensions of daily life. Via the power and healing qualities of music, people can find connections in a subculture in which they feel at home and can shape themselves into the people they want to be. This may facilitate them finding their place in society. Psytrance thus stimulates a person to become in harmony with oneself and with other psytrance-listeners. The community plays a vital role in the search for harmony and happiness, a tendency that can also be found in green, nature-oriented hippie-movements and neo-shamanistic subgroups. New insights into these growing subgroups in the Netherlands may be able to inform theoretical understandings of the current changes in Dutch society. By combining various movements to meet their own needs, youth create their own futures.

To conclude, the psytrance community as an environment for social healing via music can improve the lives of young people who try to find their way in modern society. While we will never know for sure in which direction the world will go, some psytrance enthusiasts envision the 'power of the Goa spirit' as 'ultimately affecting all humankind' (Joshua Schmidt 2015, 131).

References

Gaia, G. 2014/2015.*Chai, Charas and Changa. Psychedelic Gnosis in Psytrance Gatherings*. Contested Knowledge. University of Amsterdam, 1-26.

De Ledesma, C. 2012. *The psytrance party*. Doctoral dissertation, University of East London.

Hutson, S. R. 1999. "Technoshamanism: spiritual healing in the rave subculture." *Popular Music & Society*, 23(3), 53-77.

Lindquist, G. 1997. *Shamanic performances on the urban scene: neo-shamanism in contemporary Sweden*. Doctoral dissertation, Stockholm University.

Moore, K., & Miles, S. 2004. "Young people, dance and the sub-cultural consumption of drugs." *Addiction Research & Theory*, 12(6), 507-523.

Pini, M., 2001. *Club Cultures & Female Subjectivity*. Basingstoke, UK: Palgrave

Rouget, G. 1985. *Music and trance: A theory of the relations between music and possession*. University of Chicago Press.

Samuel, G. 1995. "Performance, Vision and Transformation in Shamanic Ritual: Healers, Clients and Societies." *Shamanism in Performing Arts. T. Kim, M. Hoppál and O. Sadovszky, eds*, 253-262.

Schmidt, J. 2015. "Goa: 20 Years of Psychedelic Trance." *Dancecult: Journal of Electronic Dance Music Culture, 7*(1), 129-131.

Sidky, H. 2009. "A shaman's cure: the relationship between altered states of consciousness and shamanic healing." *Anthropology of Consciousness, 20*(2), 171-197.

St John, G. 2018. "The breakthrough experience: DMT hyperspace and its liminal aesthetics." *Anthropology of Consciousness, 29*(1), 57-76.

St John, G. 2019. *The local scenes and global culture of psytrance*. Routledge. *Music Culture, 1*(1).

Sylvan, R. 2002. *Traces of the spirit: The religious dimensions of popular music*. NYU Press.

Tramacchi, Des. 2006. "Vapours and Visions: Religious Dimensions of DMT Use". PhD thesis, School of History, Philosophy, Religion and Classics, University of Queensland.

Vedava, P. 2015. "Exploring Psytrance as Technognosis: A Hypothesis of Participation." In *Exploring Psychedelic Trance and Electronic Dance Music in Modern Culture* (pp. 170-205). IGI Global.

Wallis, R. J. 2000. "Queer shamans: auto-archaeology and neo-shamanism." *World Archaeology, 32*(2), 252-262.

Wolputte, S. V. 2004. "Hang on to yourself: Of bodies, embodiment, and selves." *Annu. Rev. Anthropol., 33*, 251-269.

Art and the Otherworld: visualizing the invisible

Wouter Welling

In 1917, the German sociologist Max Weber (1864-1920), borrowing from Friedrich Schiller, used the phrase 'the disenchantment of the world' to describe the rationality characteristic of the Western worldview. From the Enlightenment on, those in the West began to rationally explain and order the world and their existence. This disenchantment, scholars have argued, goes hand in hand with a sense of discontent. Max Horkheimer and Theodor Adorno, in their *Dialectic of Enlightenment* (1944), write that man had to pay for his increase in power with a reduction in what he had power over. The 'enchanted world' was characterized by association: everything is connected to everything else, and human consciousness participates in a holistic universe. When this intrinsic relationship between humans and nature is erased by reason, an orphan-like feeling arises. Instead of association, now there is dissociation, resulting in alienation and a sense of existential loneliness. Nature changes into an 'opposite', something that can be exploited, but of which we are no longer part.

Magical thinking is based on association: fear, hope, healing, longing and spirituality are linked to materials, colours, plants, animals and stones. Magic's metaphorical language is a metonymical one, as a connection is sensed between what is desired and the material world. Magical consciousness 'is always affective, associative, and synchronistic in its mode of operation, and it is shaped through an individuals' experience within a particular environment through which meanings are gained' (Greenwood and Goodwin 2017, xv). In this way, magic is closely related to visual art.

Several recent exhibitions and publications indicate that there is a growing interest in the intimate relationship between the visual arts and spirituality. While landmark exhibitions such as *The Spiritual in Art – Abstract Painting 1890-1985* (Los Angeles County Museum of Art, 1987) and *Okkultismus und Avantgarde – Von Munch bis Mondrian 1900-1925* (Schirn Kunsthalle Frankfurt, 1995) concentrated on Western art history, the perspective was broadened with *Magiciens de la Terre* (Paris, Centre Pompidou, 1989) and *Les Maîtres du Désordre* (Paris, Musée du Quai Branly, 2012). This last exhibition gave a global view on magical-religious art and formed the essential counterpart to William Rubin's *Primitivism in Twentieth Century Art – Affinity of the Tribal and the Modern* (New York, Museum of Art, 1984). The *Primitivism* exhibit focused on the outward, the formal influence of non-Western art on Western modernists, while in the case of *Les Maîtres du Désordre* the inner, the mental correspondence was at the core, a crucial step further. Not only has visual art (whether or not that concept was in order from an emic point of view) been a means worldwide to express human relationships with a transcendental dimension, the images themselves are closely related. A sense of the magical world is universal, though the forms of expression can be culturally determined and therefore different. Furthermore, contemporary artists draw their inspiration from different sources; they incorporate elements from various cultures into their own specific visual language. In this contribution only ten of the participating artists in the *Healing Power* exhibition could be included. They all have a spiritual dimension in their work and in some cases have even been initiated into specific spiritual traditions.

More than any other form of art, performance art connects to shamanic traditions and has a strong ritual character. With his socially engaged work as an artist and as a teacher, **Joseph Beuys** (Germany, 1921-1986) was committed to a long-term process of healing. After the Second World War, Germany had a profound need for *Vergangenheitsbewältigung* (coming to terms with the past). Beuys used shamanic/alchemical methods and archetypes; the energetic dimensions of materials like honey and grease, felt and copper; and the spiritual dimension of animals like hare, deer and coyote to broaden the concept of art. He placed a honey pump in the Documenta in Kassel, melded a (copy of) the crown of a Tsar into a golden hare – just in order to make change: to change the lives of individuals (his audience, his pupils) and society as a whole.

His performance *I Like America and America Likes Me* belongs among the most famous works of art of the second half of the twentieth century. In 1974, directly after arriving in New York by plane, Beuys let himself, wrapped in felt, be transported in an ambulance – as a 'sick person' in need of healing – to the recently opened René Block gallery. He stayed there behind a fence for three days, eight hours per day, in the presence of a coyote. By doing so, he wished to restore the relationship with 'the strange and the other', the coyote, an animal considered a threat by the colonists and a sacred animal by the First Nations. The video recording of the performance – with the now-iconic image of the artist wrapped in felt, like a tent, with the 'shaman staff' sticking out – clearly shows a growing relationship between man and animal, or, better said, what Beuys in anthroposophical terms called the coyote's 'Gruppenseele' (literally translated: 'the soul of the group', the characteristics rather than the individual animal [Sünner 2015, 80]).

Healing the individual and society, ritual cleansing, and victory over hate, pain and grief are important topics in **Marina Abramović**'s oeuvre (former Yugoslavia, 1946). She has long been fascinated by energy and how it is passed on to others (Abramović 2016, 282), and energy as a regenerative force, and has researched various shamanic traditions. Her work engages with the energy of people, animals, stones (using purple amethyst, for example, in *Shoes for Departure – Transitory Objects for Human Use*) and other objects. During a 1995 performance at the Pitt Rivers Museum in Oxford, she held her hands above various magical objects from the museum's collection in order to feel their energy. A highlight in her oeuvre is the performance *The Artist is Present* (MoMA, New York, 2010). From March 14 until May 31, six days a week during the opening hours of the museum, she sat on a chair across from one museum visitor at a time, and looked them in the eyes. She was dressed in alternately a red, white and dark blue dress. During the 736.5 hours she sat there, more than 1,675 people looked her into the eyes. For many it was an unforgettable

Figure 79a *The artist is present* by Marina Abramović. Video registration of the performance in MoMA, New York, 2010. Courtesy Marina Abramović Institute.

Figure 79b *The artist is present* by Marina Abramović in the exhibition *Healing Power*, Leiden 2019. Photo: Ben Bekooy.

experience. To be truly emotionally open to another, hour after hour, day after day, is an Olympic achievement.

In her work, **Mathilde ter Heijne** (France, 1969) integrates the working methods and other aspects of archaeology, anthropology and sociology. Many historical, cultural and gender-specific elements influence the way we experience ourselves and the world around us. In her work, Ter Heijne searches for alternatives, for new points of view. One way she operates is by researching and participating in various forms of magical consciousness, from European witchcraft to African Vodun. One of her works, *Drawing down the moon* (2006), is named after a witches' invocation to the moon goddess. In it, a life-size bronze cast of Ter Heijne, depicted as a high priestess in the European neo-pagan witchcraft tradition, is joined by the sound of a woman's voice singing the cantata. The sculpture is naked (in witchcraft, it is not unusual to perform rituals 'skyclad'), wearing only a body stocking, whose net design is reminiscent of the snakeskin, the serpent being one of the prehistoric great goddess's sacred animals (Gimbutas 1991, 124). The serpent is a liminal symbol par excellence – the in-between of good and evil, life and death – and is also related to the goddess of magic and witchcraft, Hecate. Ter Heijne's installation *Send it back to where it came from* (2010) refers as well to witchcraft through its use of candles. In this interactive installation, just as in a church, the visitor can buy a candle, light it and place it in a wide metal bowl. Only this time lighting the candle is not part of making a request to a saint, but used in a reversal spell: the candles are black, and underneath the wax is red, so when lit they become slowly covered with red drippings. On the candle are letters in gold, in which the problem, the obstacle one would like to get rid of, is written: patriarchy, misogyny, ownership etc. In this presentation their phallic form placed in the bowl could also be interpreted as the union of opposites, male and female.

Just like someone who receives a calling to become a shaman and first rejects it, but eventually accepts the heavy burden of this task, so **Johan Tahon** (Belgium, 1965) describes his profession as an artist. 'In any case', he writes, 'I'm sure to have done everything not to have to be an artist, but there was no other option. I was forced to do and undergo what I undergo now' (Tahon 2016, 9). Tahon feels an affinity with shamanism, with the pain and the transforming power involved in it, going so far as to acquire an old shamanic costume. His sculpture *Fin* (2004-2014), with a height of more than three meters, seems to be a spiritual traveller who is inseparably connected to a shamanic ladder. He is in a liminal phase, about to leave the earthly, material realm.

Tahon has travelled through the unconscious; dreams convey images to him. From the age of fourteen he studied the work of C. G. Jung. In his sculptures white has a strong presence, both in plaster and glaze. He mostly creates vertical figures expressing vulnerability and incompleteness, though they also convey an intrinsic

Figure 80a Mathilde ter Heijne lightens the candles of her work *Send it back to where it came from*, 2010. Leiden, 28 juni 2019. Photo: Wouter Welling.

Figure 80b. *Send it back where it came from* by Mathilde ter Heijne, 2010. Metal, wax, 150 x 125 x 125 cm. Collection of the artist. Photo: Christine Dierenbach.

strength. The intention is not to present a perfect outside, but an inside visualizing itself in an anguished form. The sculptures are 'inside out' and the inside is connected to an immaterial realm that insists on manifestation.

Figure 81 Exhibition room *Between worlds* in the exhibition *Healing Power*, Leiden 2019. At the left *Fin* by Johan Tahon, 2004-2014, plaster. Photo: Ben Bekooy.

Figure 82 *Imposición de manos* (*Laying on of hands*) by José Bedia, U.S.A., ca.2013. Pigment on amate paper, 121 x 242 cm.. NMVW no. AM-708-1. Photo: Irene de Groot.

José Bedia (Cuba, 1950) is a Palo Monte priest who draws inspiration as an artist from the rich concepts and imagery of that originally Cuban religion with Congo roots. The artist was initiated into the Sioux religion as well. His interest is directed to any form of magical-religious experience, and he is a great collector of tribal art. His drawing *Imposición de manos* (*Laying on of hands*, ca. 2013) is executed on *amate* paper, a type of paper made with layers on layers, to which shamans of the Pueblo people attribute magical qualities. The hands, completely out of proportion, reach out for the spiritual realm and transfer healing power.

Healing is an essential theme in the work of the African American artist **Renée Stout** (United States, 1958). She has researched the African diaspora religions, especially the magical-religious herbal healing method of Obeah. Stout's work expresses strength and the possibility of positive change in a visually poetic manner. About her work *Incantation #6 (The Alchemy of Healing)*, 2015, she writes: 'As an artist I keep wondering what magic or energy being transformed "looks" like as it is occurring. *I was trying to visualize what can't be seen*' (Stout, email 2017). Visualizing the invisible, the working of energy, she created this work after a close friend had ended her life. The work is, as the title indicates, an incantation of sorrow and loss. The numbers 3-21 in the painting refer to the date of the passing of her friend, she

Figure 83 *Incantation #6 – The Alchemy of Healing* by Renée Stout, 2015. Acrylic on canvas, glass, rhinestones. 45,7 x 180,3 x 0,3 cm. Courtesy Renée Stout & Hemphill Gallery, Washington DC. NMVW no. 7164-1a. Photo: Irene de Groot.

explains: 'It was a way for me to visualize healing energy and in my mind the act of painting it was putting healing energy out into the world' (ibid.). The painting shows a bleeding hart, with drops of blood trailing down to the floor where they are crystalized into rhinestones in a puddle of bloody red glass. Blood, transformation and the shining stones symbolize the alchemical process and an imperishable energy.

Santiago Rodríguez Olazábal (Cuba, 1955) is a Regla de Ifá priest, one of the African diaspora religions. He consults the Ifá oracle to advise his clients with their problems. In the installation *Yo me lo llevo viento malo* (*I take the evil wind with me*, 1998) we see an Ifá priest, a *babalawo*, drawn on the right, cleansing his client, on the left, with magical dust, the potency of which is enhanced by blowing it over a beam with powerful objects attached to it. The broom on the beam is a reference to Congolese traditions. There, a *mpiya* may be used, which is a broom animated by a deceased family member, to treat a disease or turn away evil influences. The act takes place at a crossroads: traditionally the place for sacrifice, for connecting with the Otherworld. Hence the crossroads made of earth in front of the two- and three-dimensional scene.

Remy Jungerman (Moengo, Surinam, 1959) developed a visual language connecting two cultures: Surinamese and Dutch. In his installations he fuses references to Winti rituals and Marron textiles with elements from modernists such as Mondrian and Malevitch. Marrons were people forced into slavery on the plantations; they succeeded in escaping from slavery and fled to the outback, developing a culture with a rich spirituality. Signs and symbols from that culture appear in *Bakru*, an installation named after the anything but friendly 'gnome' in the centre of the installation. Bakru is a Winti (spirit) from the forest, a potentially threatening or at least unreliable force from the wilderness. The mask he wears evokes the African roots of the Marrons. The trellis defining the composition of the installation is partially covered with maps of the Netherlands, and the offerings made to Bakru are mostly of Dutch origin as well. The horizontal and vertical slats refer to Mondrian's compositions. Just like Stout's and Olazábal's installations Jungerman's work combines two- and the three-dimensional materials, associating objects and images, and defining itself between matter and mind. It is exactly in this elusive realm that contemporary art related to spirituality is situated.

References

Gimbutas, San Francisco. 1991. *The Language of the Goddess*, San Francisco: Harper.

Greenwood, Susan, Erik D. Goodwyn. 2017. *Magical Consciousness – An Anthropological and Neurobiological Approach*, New York & London: Routledge.

Stout, Renée. 2017. Email to the author, 28 February.

Sünner, Rüdiger. 2015. *Zeige deine Wunde – Kunst und Spiritualität bei Joseph Beuys*, Berlin: Europa Verlag.

Tahon, Johan. 2016. *Adorant*, Tielt: Lannoo.

About the authors

Claudia Augustat was awarded her PhD from the Goethe University in Frankfurt. She worked at the Weltkulturen Museum in Frankfurt a.M. and at the Ethnological Museum in Berlin before she became the curator for South American Collections at the Weltmuseum Wien in 2004. From 2015 to 2017, she was the curatorial project manager for the refurbishment of the Weltmuseum Wien. In 2019 she became the leader of the project "Taking Care" co-founded by the commission of the European Union. Her research focuses on Amazonian collections from the 19th century, material culture and cultural memory, on collaborative curatorship and the decolonization of museum praxis.

Markus Balkenhol is an anthropologist at the Meertens Institute, Amsterdam, working on issues of colonialism, race, citizenship, cultural heritage, and religion. His PhD thesis, 'Tracing Slavery: An Ethnography of Diaspora, Affect, and Cultural Heritage in Amsterdam' (cum laude, 2014) deals with cultural memories of slavery in Amsterdam. His most recent publications include: 'Iconic Objects: Making Diasporic Heritage, Blackness and Whiteness in the Netherlands', in Birgit Meyer and Mattijs van de Port (eds), Sense and Essence: Heritage and the Cultural Production of the Real (Berghahn Books, 2018); and 'Silence and the Politics of Compassion: Commemorating Slavery in the Netherlands', Social Anthropology/Antropologie Sociale 23(4) (2016).

Ulrike Bohnet is an anthropologist and museum professional. Her MA field research focused on the return of shamanism in Post-socialism in Tywa, South Siberia where she compared contemporary shamanism in Siberia, Russian Far East and Scandinavia. Ulrike Bohnet is interested in the connection of contemporary shamanic worldviews, material culture/art and cultural identities. She has curated exhibitions about these multi-layered topics in international teams, collaborating with students and artists at the Ethnologisches Museum Berlin (2003), Adelshauser Museum Freiburg (2006), Lindenmuseum in Stuttgart (2007-2009), Stiftung Museum Schloss Moyland (2021).

Cunera Buijs is anthropologist and curator Arctic of the National Museum of World Cultures, Leiden. Her research interest lies in issues of dress and identity, and questions of ownership, authority and access. In 2004, she finished her PhD-thesis on clothing, its significance and role in Inuit society (Leiden University). Her publications have also focused on climate change, the trade boycott of sealskin. Cunera's most recent publications include Living objects, The transfer of knowledge through East Greenlandic material culture, in: *Traditions, Traps and Trends, Transfer of Knowledge in Arctic Regions,* Jarich Oosten and Barbara Miller (eds), UAP's Polynya Press, 2018, pp. 143-189 and Shared Inuit Culture: Museums and Arctic Communities from a European Perspective, *Etudes/Inuit/Studies* Vol. 41 (1), in: *Collections arctiques/ Arctic Collections,* 2018, Gwénaëlle Guignon & Aurélie Maire (eds.), pp. 37-61. She is co-organizer of the exhibition *Healing Power, Winti, shamanism and more* (2019).

Maria van Daalen has an MA in Dutch Literature and Linguistics and she is a Dutch poet/artist and writer who has published eight volumes of poetry, a book of stories, two translations (Italian poetry, and 14th-century Flemish-Dutch courtly poetry) and a famous academic article on a manuscript of Orlando di Lasso. She is a *Manbo Asogwe* in Haitian Vodou (since 2007) and belongs as such to the international congregation *Société La Fraicheur Belle Fleur Guinea (Port-au-Prince/New Orleans).*

Anatoly Donkan was born in Tunguska in Siberia. As a Nanai artist, he lives and works both in St. Petersburg, Russia and in Viechtach, Germany. He studied in Khabarovsk and graduated in 1992 with a degree in Graphic Art and Education. His work is inspired by Nanai traditions and Nanai museum collections. He works predominantly with tanned fish skins, wood carving, blacksmithing and painting. In 2019-2020, Anatoly Donkan had a solo exhibition at the State Museum of Anthropology in St. Petersburg. His work is part of several European museum collections and is also exhibited in the *Healing Power* exhibition in the Tropenmuseum in Amsterdam in 2021-2022.

Peter Geschiere is emeritus professor for the Anthropology of Africa at both the University of Amsterdam and Leiden University; he is also co-editor of ETHNOGRAPHY (SAGE). Since 1971 he has undertaken historical-anthropological fieldwork in various parts of Cameroon and elsewhere in West and Central Africa. His publications include *The Modernity of Witchcraft: Politics and the Occult in Post-colonial Africa* (Univ. Of Virginia Press, 1997), *Perils of Belonging: Autochthony, Citizenship and Exclusion in Africa and Europe* (Univ. of Chicago Press, 2009), *Witchcraft, Intimacy and Trust: Africa in Comparison* (Univ. of Chicago Press, 2013) and 'A "Vortex of Identities" – Freemasonry, Witchcraft and Post-colonial Homophobia in Cameroon,' *African Studies Review* 60(2), 2017, p. 7-35.

Susan Greenwood is an anthropologist and a past Visiting Senior Research Fellow at the University of Sussex, and a former Lecturer and Visiting Fellow at Goldsmiths, University of London. Her books include *Magical Consciuousness: An Anthropological and Neurobiological Approach,* (with Erik. D.Goodwyn), (Routlegde, 2017) and *Developing Magical Consciousness: a theoretical and practical guide for the expansion of perception* (Routlegde, 2019). She lectures internationally.

Iris Hesse holds a MA cultural Anthropology at the University of Leiden. During her study she specialised in visual anthropology and conducted research among the Rotori's, a group of young Dutch students who organize psytrance dance festivals in the Netherlands. She has a great interest in subculture studies and alternative forms of living in our current Western society, which formed her research. Furthermore, music is a great passion of hers, which she expresses through film. She is now working on an anthropological film project in Australia, which centers on music and culture.

Sebastiaan van 't Holt has a BA in cultural anthropology at Leiden university. While studying he developed an interest in the contemporary use of psychedelic substances: their social and cultural context, their link to modern psychiatry and society in general, the current legal issues regarding these plants and their reference to artistic expression. First in the Netherlands, and later on in Peru. During his MA study in 2018 he conducted field research among Shipibo, their shamans and tourists visiting the area. He collected contemporary artefacts for the Museum of World Cultures.

Daan van Kampenhout, originally a textile artist (with shaman/ritual costumes as graduation project in 1986/7), was a personal student of Lakota, Southern Ute and Sámi teachers. Daan works worldwide as a teacher in contemporary shamanic practice, he has published 7 books and his writings have been translated into 12 languages.

Marian Markelo is a teacher nursery at the ROC Mondriaan in Delft. She is active in welfare in the Hague, Rotterdam and Amsterdam. In 1984, she was initiated as a Winti healer and she is a specialist in African-Surinamese social, cultural, historical and religious heritage. From the 1990s, she organizes educational activities, together with the 'Sisters van Maat' Henna Linger and Shirley Noter in Amsterdam Zuid-Oost. Marian Markelo organizes heritage-journeys in the Netherlands, Ghana, Benin and Surinam. Since 2014, she is a member of the board at NiNSee (knowledge center for the slavery past). She was also board-member of the foundation for the commemoration and celebration of the 150 years of abolition of trans-Atlantic slavery.

Barbara Helen Miller is an independent scholar and Jungian psychoanalyst. Graduate of the C. G. Jung Institute, Zürich, she holds the Master of Arts in Psychology and Religion and Ph.D. in Anthropology from Leiden University. She conducted research among the Coastal Sámi of the Porsanger area in Northern Norway, studying the pre-Christian and shamanic Sámi religions, as well as, Christian Laestadianism, a pietistic movement among the Sámi. In her dissertation *Connecting and Correcting* (2007) Barbara provides an emic image of the perception of her Sámi-informants, related to Sámi healing and transfer of knowledge. Barbara lives in Hilversum.

Terto Ngiviu studied history and culture at the University of Greenland. She specialized in the semantics of clothing and spirituality. Recently she conducts PhD research at the University of Cambridge on spirituality, shamanism and Christianity in Inuit culture of Northern Greenland. Terto lives in Nuuk.

Sigvald Persen is from Sámi descent and lives in Northern Norway. Manager of the Sámi cultural centre in Indre Billefjord, he is active in research related to Sámi identity, place names, language and culture. From his mother Nanna, a Sámi healer, he inherited the gift of healing and advice. Sigvald treats people predominantly by cupping but uses also other techniques. He considers the most important is to listen, thereby taking care of what people tell. Sigvald Persen has an extensive knowledge on Sámi-Christian and pre-Christian spiritual culture and healing traditions.

Juan Carlos Reyes Gómez is from Ayuuk (or Mixe) descent (in Oaxaca, Mexico), and he is a linguist. He completed his licenciatura studies at Escuela Nacional de Antropología e Historia and a master's degree at Centro de Investigaciones y Estudios Superiores en Antropología Social, in Mexico city. Recently, he completed his doctoral studies at the Faculty of Archaeology of Leiden University, in the Netherlands, under the supervision of Prof. Dr. Maarten Jansen.
Juan Carlos has been a teacher and researcher in different institutions in Mexico. The subjects that he has worked from teaching and research are: linguistics, sociolinguistics, literacy, intercultural bilingual education, Ayuuk oral literature, ayuuk calendar, ayuuk religion and worldview and linguistic and cultural rights of indigenous peoples.

Coby Rijkers is a micro-biologist, teacher biology at a secundary school and she is a Dutch witch. Inspired by the farmer's cultural background of her ancestors, she started to study the history and contemporary use of witchcraft and healing in the Netherlands. It turned out that this (local) knowledge almost disappeared. Therefore, she added information and (scientific) knowledge from the British *Museum of*

Witchcraft and Magic in Boscastle. She is officially initiated as a witch. She established a school for traditional witchcraft and Dutch folklore 'De wolderse heks' and helps people with her knowledge of spirituality, healing and nature.

Reimar Schefold is professor emeritus Cultural Anthropology and Sociology of Indonesia at Leiden University. He has a long-standing interest in thematic symbolic anthropology, art, vernacular architecture, and social change among ethnic minorities. He has conducted several extensive periods of fieldwork in Indonesia, notably among the Sakuddei of Siberut, Mentawai Islands, where he spent two years from 1967 to 1969 and several shorter stays later; the Batak of Sumatra, and the Sa'dan Toraja of Sulawesi. He is editor and one of the authors of *Eyes of the ancestors: the arts of island Southeast Asia at the Dallas Museum of Art* (Dallas: Dallas Museum of Art; New Haven etcetera: Yale University Press. 2013) and, with Han F. Vermeulen, of *Treasure hunting? Collectors and collections of Indonesian artefacts* (Leiden: Reseach School CNWS/National Museum of Ethnology. 2002). His most recent publication is *Toys for the souls: life and art on the Mentawai Islands* (Belgium: Primedia sprl. 2017) where in the Bibliography more of his writings on Mentawai can be found. Reimar Schefold can be reached at: schefold@kpnmail.nl.

David Stuart-Fox was a longtime resident in Bali in the 1970s and 1980s. He received his Ph.D. from the Australian National University in 1987. From 1991 to 2013 he was librarian at Museum Volkenkunde in Leiden.

Wouter Welling is curator contemporary art at the National Museum of World Cultures. Since the 80s he has been working as an art critic and curator, mainly in the field of globalization and interculturality in the art world. He has published numerous articles, books and catalogues about both western and non-western art, such as *Ad Fontes! An intercultural search for hidden sources* (2001), *Kijken zonder Grenzen – hedendaagse kunst in het Afrika Museum, de collectie Valk en verder* (2006), *Roots & More – The Journey of the Spirits (*with Irene Hübner, 2009), *Dangerous and Divine – the secret of the serpent* (2012), a Jungian approach to serpent symbolism. He has a special interest in esotericism and occultism in the visual arts. He curated solo exhibitions such as *The Dono Code* (Heri Dono, Tropenmuseum, 2009) and *Abdoulaye Konate* (Afrika Museum, 2013). He is co-curator of the exhibition *Healing Power, Winti, shamanism and more* (2019).